ready2dress

ready2dress

ready2dress

HOW TO HAVE STYLE WITHOUT FOLLOWING FASHION

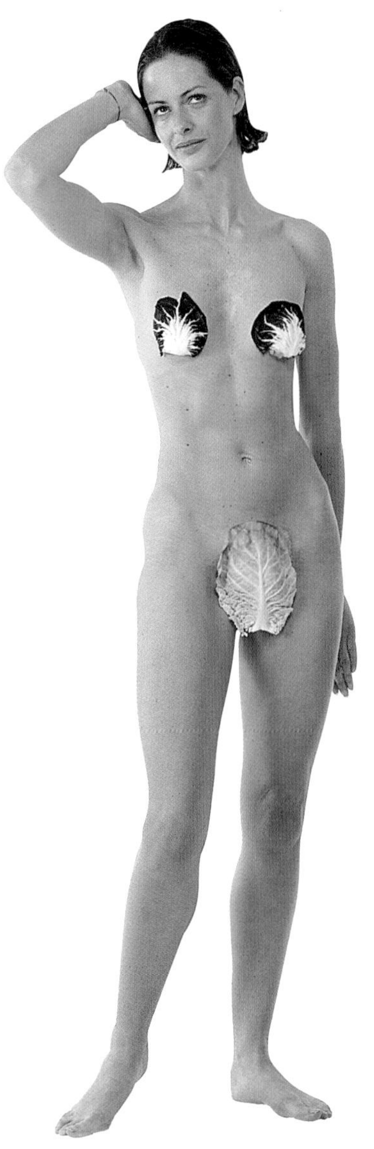

SUSANNAH CONSTANTINE
&
TRINNY WOODALL

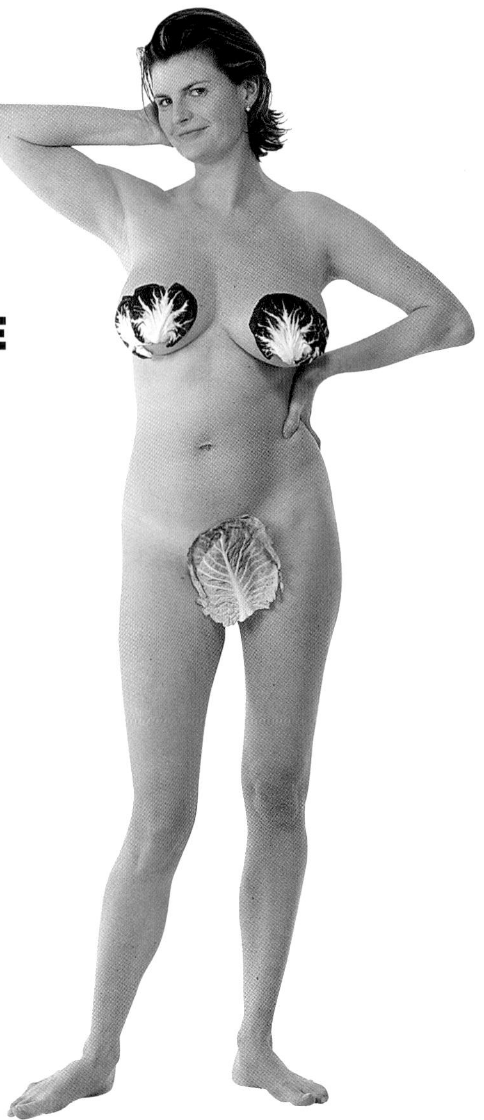

CASSELL&CO

First published in the United Kingdom in 2000 by Cassell & Co

A CIP catalogue record for this book is available from the British Library

ISBN 0 304 35425 2

Photography by Edward Sykes

Design Director **David Rowley**
Editorial Director **Susan Haynes**

Designer **Nigel Soper**
Editor **Maggie Ramsay**
Typeset in Helvetica Neue
Printed in Italy

Cassell & Co
Wellington House
125 Strand
London WC2R 0BB

DEDICATION

To Jonny Too Bad, Sten, Eric Baily, who gave us our first break, and Al Lowman, who is making it all happen.

CONTENTS

Fat stomach,
what fat stomach?

INTRODUCTION

'Elegance is innate… it has nothing to do with being well dressed'

DIANA VREELAND

What a load of bollocks. How you dress makes a huge difference to how other people perceive you and, therefore, treat you: with respect, admiration, or contempt. However, dressing to look your best is not about following fashion or spending wads of cash on what's hip for the season. If you've got fat, pitted thighs no miniskirt, however gorgeous, is going to flatter you.

Unfortunately, there are women out there who are oblivious to their defects and appalling sense of style. As this type of woman won't be buying this book for herself, we appeal to her friends to buy it for her. You will be doing yourself a favour by taking away the ghastly embarrassment of having to sit through lunch with someone who looks like the combined audience of an Oprah Winfrey show.

We do, however, realize that the world is made up of a great many body shapes, so we searched the globe and found Normandy, Lorna, Joanna and Rosemary. Between the six of us, we can zero in on most of the bodily defects known to woman. And we can show how to deal with them.

STYLE IS...

- not something you are born with, but something everyone can learn.
- mixing and matching.
- wearing something no one else has.
- combining different hues of one colour.
- being aware that expensive clothes do not automatically make you stylish.
- remembering that something that makes your friend look fabulous will not necessarily work for you.
- understanding which shapes are appropriate for you and which to avoid. You will be able to build on this framework and acquire your individuality through your accessories. You might become known for the great rings you wear or the unusual bags you collect. It's all a part of saying 'I'm not a sheep.'

1

HOW TO MAKE THE MOST OF YOURSELF

INTRODUCTION

You are about to see us in the buff, and many of you will think: 'What have they got to worry about? They are both tall and slim.' Well, like most women, although we may be aware of our good points, we tend to focus on our bad ones. No matter what our size or shape, we all have insecurities about certain parts, but it's important to remember that what you hate about yourself could well be the envy of your best friend.

Looking stylish begins with an honest appraisal of what we like and loathe about our bodies. This means standing naked in front of a mirror and taking stock. What are we always trying to hide? Can we bare our flabby arms in a sleeveless dress? Do our thick ankles look better or worse in ankle-strap shoes? If our buttocks don't fit in the mirror, should we be wearing skin-clinging trousers?

Once you have established that maybe your hefty shoulders in strappy dresses make you look like a transvestite, or that rock-chick roots look decidedly tacky in the real world, dressing well and looking good will become second nature.

Who said 'red and green should never be seen'?

A quick leaf through this book and you'll soon wise up

NORMANDY

big-breasted fashion victim

Here we have a chick who dresses to compete with her girlfriends. Her name is at the top of every designer store's waiting list, first in line to show off the newest fad. In her mind, owning the latest Gucci mule or Prada bag is being at the front of cutting edge design. Her idea of living dangerously is the possibility of turning up for dinner in the same dress as her hostess.

She's usually decked from head to toe in one designer, not out of label loyalty, but because she does not have the sense of style to mix and match. The fact that she believes cheap is nasty and the high street is for those without style reveals her total lack of inspiration. She is the kind of girl to gush over your shoes, only to be disappointed at discovering they came from a chain store.

Obsessed with her appearance and an imperfection phobic, a rogue pubic hair left after a wax will ruin her day.

She's young, she's slim, she has an amazing pair of tits – so what's her problem? Well, for a start, we can imagine that buying dresses, suits and coats that fit both top and bottom halves of her body is going to be tricky. And while we're all in favour of a girl making the most of her natural assets, Normandy has to be careful she doesn't look top-heavy and tarty.

HOW SHE SEES HERSELF

- I have an image to uphold
- I can only wear a one-piece swimsuit because of my appendix scar
- I have no waist
- I have huge droopy tits which I hate to display
- My lips are too thin and no needle is going near them to plump them up
- My legs may be thin and long but they are bow-shaped

HOW WE SEE HER

- We see the label before we see her
- She is lucky to have had keyhole surgery
- No waist, no hips, O to be able to wear masculine-cut trousers
- Yes, they're huge, and they're not going to get any smaller, if her plastic surgery phobia is anything to go by – so don't make an exhibition of them
- Nothing that a well applied lipstick won't change
- They're thin – let go of their shape

NORMANDY

Worst looks

- Cropped cardigan – leads eye to thick waist
- Round-neck vest – makes chest look like one big saggy lump
- Halter necks: tits creep out either side
- Waisted trousers: top of trouser is too close to drooping boobs, leaving no room to define waist with layering
- Tight drainpipes – serve only to enhance the bow of her legs

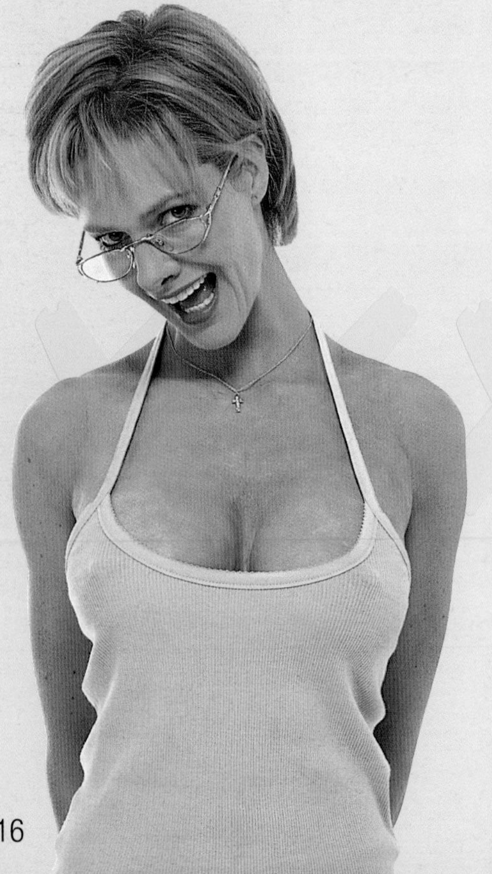

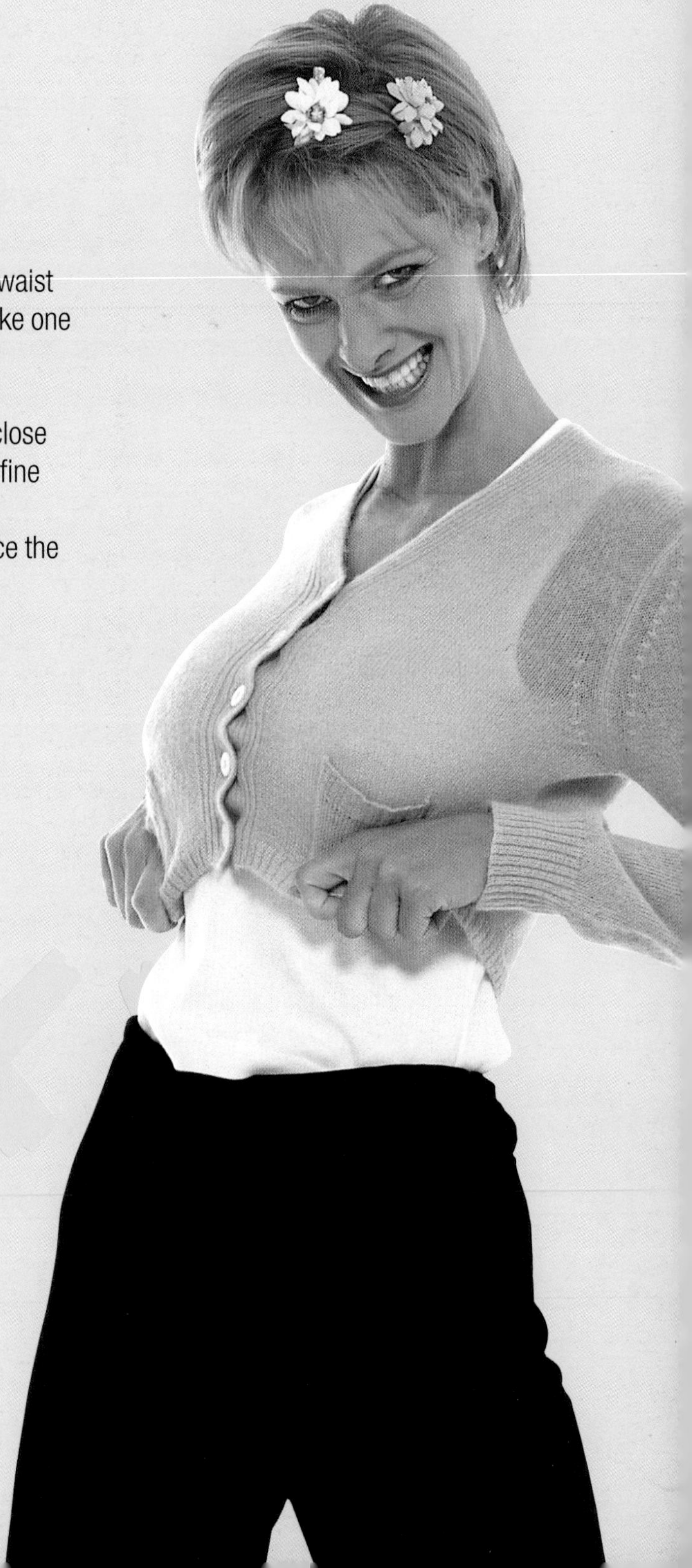

Best looks

- Long line cotton cardigan unbuttoned up to the waist will make narrow hips look more voluptuous
- V-neck sleeveless T-shirts: the V breaks up the expanse of her chest and no sleeves show off her toned arms
- Sports bra under T-shirts to minimize size and sag
- Cocktail dress with low draw-string neckline: the gathers help to dwarf size of chest
- Hipster trousers make hips look wider and therefore waist look smaller
- Palazzo pants or loose bootleg trousers, so nothing clings to those bow legs
- Wide leg trousers balance top-heavy titties, while a co-ordinating shawl pulls the whole look together

LORNA

young mum stuck in a rut

Lorna is in her late 20s (but looks 40), with two kids. During the day she wears her husband's big T-shirt and skintight leggings that reveal her cellulite, even in darker shades. The rolls of fat have crept on gradually over the past seven or eight years – she accepts them as part of growing older.

Her hair is disastrous, with roots on show and a perm that has never quite grown out.

In her mind, the brighter the make-up, the more glamorous the effect. The same applies to clothing. She will inevitably ruin a pair of simple black trousers with gaudy pumps, or wreck a plain navy T-shirt dress by drenching it in gold jewellery and a fake Versace belt.

Children rule the housekeeping budget, leaving little for Lorna to spend on herself. Unfortunately, she believes that designer labels automatically equal chic and stylish, which leads her to live in a time warp, clinging on four seasons later to the strongest, least attractive fashion statements, such as Chanel's gold chain era.

HOW SHE SEES HERSELF

• My husband's pet name for me is thunder thighs
• My tits squidge under my arms
• The rolls of fat on my stomach make my husband feel seasick
• I hate my mousy hair, and make the most effort to be blond, but I am always getting bad roots
• Please, someone, give me a solution to stop biting my nails

HOW WE SEE HER

• She has the basics to be beautiful
• We understand that childbirth can do terrible things to the body, but we know plenty of women who have summoned up all their willpower to turn themselves around, shape up and stun the world
• She's wearing the wrong shaped bra
• She wears clothes that only enhance what she most wants to hide
• Her colouring would be far better suited to auburn
• Her nails let her down every time

LORNA

Worst looks

- Jackets ending on or above her backside will only exaggerate its width
- Long dresses cut on the bias make thunderous thighs positively torpedo-like
- Man's shape trousers with pockets cut into the side seam will always be too big on the waist and too tight on the hips
- Trousers with pleats will be pulled and stretched, acting as a dead giveaway to the fat underneath
- Clinging dresses – have too many lumps and bumps to cling to

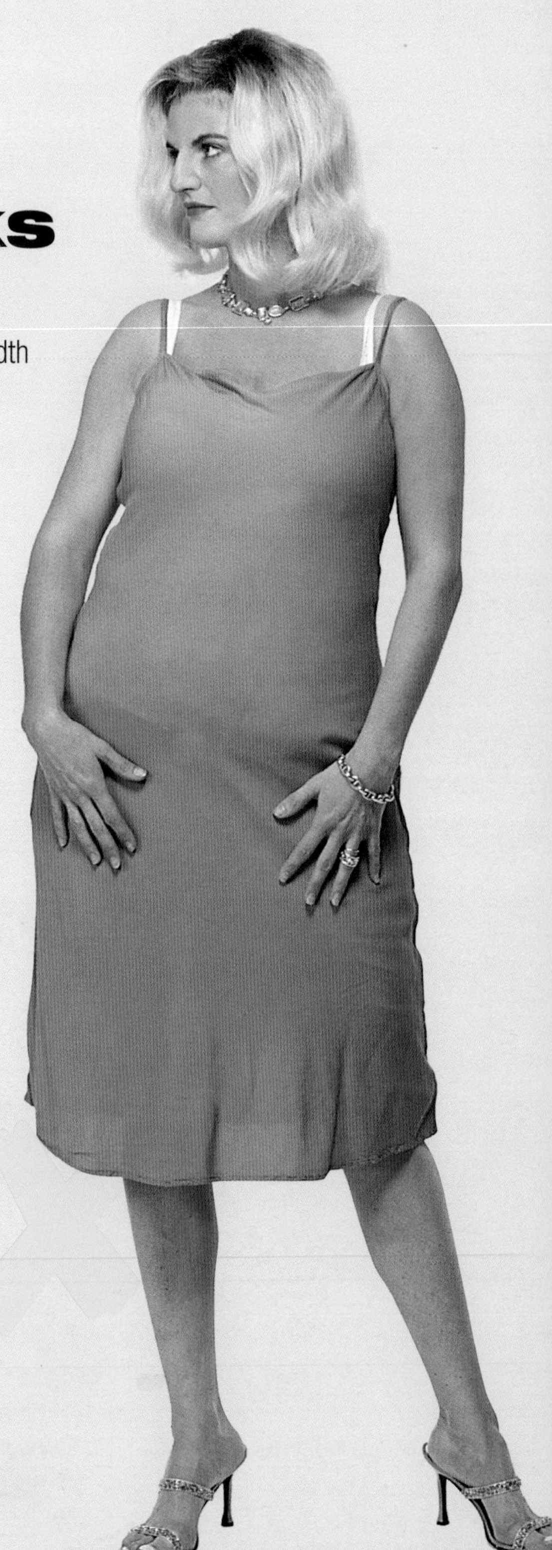

Best looks

- A jumper tied around the waist when wearing trousers splits up expanse of rear end
- A-line skirts that hang away from the leg
- Knee-length jackets that cover up all sins
- Structured shoulders to balance disproportionate hip size
- Skirts or dresses with a frilled hem give a sense of harmony to those child-bearing hips
- Wearing one colour from top to toe elongates and slims by drawing the eye up and down, not across the width

TRINNY

flat-chested, short-legged craterface

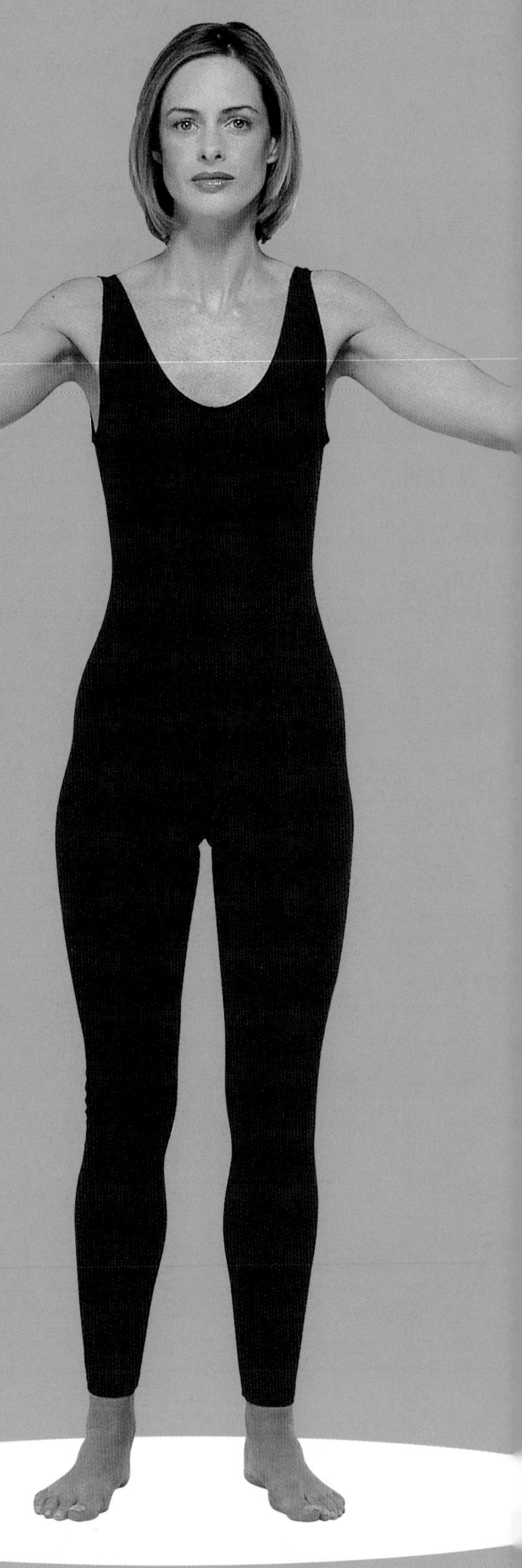

People think that Trinny is one of that rare breed of women who were born with an innate knowledge of how to dress. She knows that the real story lies in years of dedicated spending and an insecure belief that you are what you wear.

Her style is worked on weekly. Monthly culls take place in her wardrobe. Trousers that were favourites one week are murdered the next. There is no room for sentimentality in the cupboard of T Woodall. If it doesn't suit, it doesn't survive.

Like a hypochondriac who loves to play doctor, her fear of looking ugly is translated to her friends with remarkable results, as she drags them to her box of tricks for a quick makeover.

Her confidence is not a family trait. It was self-taught. Many will remember her New Romantic phase before the butterfly emerged. This incorporated long damask jackets and drainpipe trousers finished off with large earrings and a trilby. Individual, yes. Stylish, no.

Fake tan was also a winner during the 1980s. Orange was her colour, often streaked and darker around the eyebrows and elbows. Coupled with pearly pink lipstick this made for a Sloane longing to break into the heady realms of Tramp and Eurotrash.

Today her dress sense is just as eye-catching, but thankfully in a more refined way. She knows exactly how to dress to make the best of herself and even if her life depended on it, she will never again be seen in a pair of high-waisted trousers.

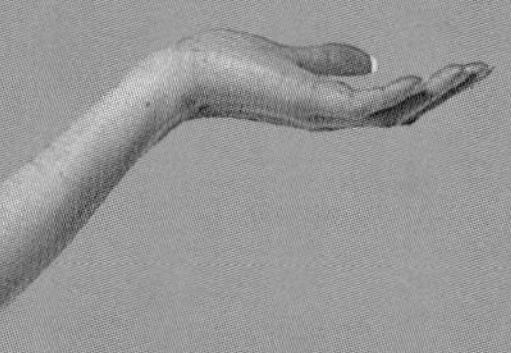

HOW TRINNY SEES HERSELF

• Acne that has left me with skin that needs polyfilling
• Stunted legs caused by pre-pubescent arrested development…
• …ending in chunky calves and thick ankles
• I wish my chest could occasionally be the reason men might talk to me
• My waist is long enough to bridge the English Channel…
• …and my low-slung bum doesn't help

HOW SUSANNAH SEES TRINNY

• She has a beautiful face, so who cares about her skin?
• Short legs don't matter when your bum is the size of a peanut – even if it's not as pert as some
• Her ankles are a problem, but that's why they invented trousers and boots
• Her pancake-flat boobs allow her to look lithe and willowy in anything
• Her stomach is as flat as her chest

TRINNY

Worst looks

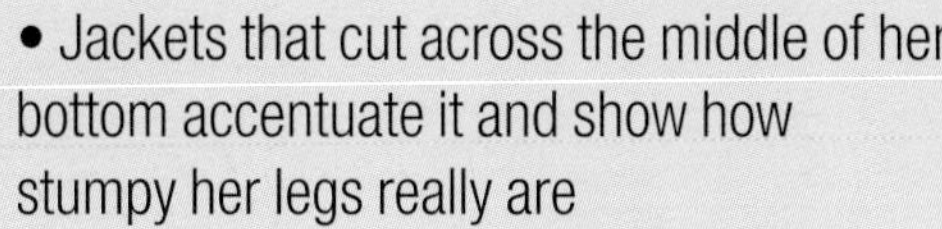

- Jackets that cut across the middle of her bottom accentuate it and show how stumpy her legs really are
- Fitted high-waisted trousers – people with a long back look terrible in waisters
- Short, loose-fitting tops that leave a gap between this and the bottom half make the lady look like a tramp
- Delicate high-heeled shoes with tight skirts; if you want to see Trin looking hideous, this is the look to go for. Unless you have incredibly thin, gorgeous legs, tight and high does nothing for you
- Dresses with a tight plunging neckline and hip-skimming skirt serve to show off all she hates about her body

Best looks

- Long line jackets that cover her ass entirely
- Long waisted tops that are very fitted, with something a little shorter worn over the top to break up her long back
- Palazzo pants with non-gathered elastic waist cover where her ass ends and waist begins, thus making her short legs appear longer
- Wearing the same colour trousers, socks and shoes will elongate the length of the legs
- A jumper tied around the waist disguises a long back and a low-slung bum
- Short trousers and dumpy shoes give a happy illusion of an elegant ankle

SUSANNAH

big-titted sumo arm wrestler

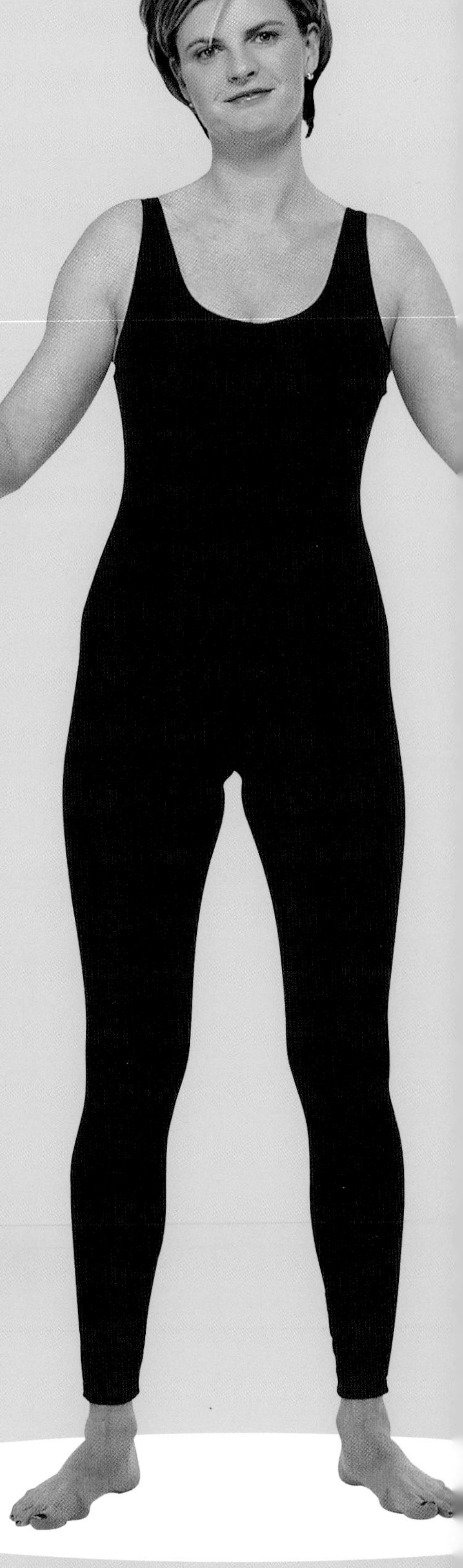

As a child, Susannah was dressed by her father, a man with immaculate taste and an eye only for the best. Once she was left to her own devices this borrowed style disappeared as her adolescent spots arrived. Very much a timid sheep, she followed the flock and took on the role of Sloane Ranger, relieved to be just like her friends.

In those days her biggest problem was her skinny legs. To combat teasing, she would wear eight pairs of woolly tights cut off at the knee to make her legs look fatter under trousers. This was massively uncomfortable in the heat.

Before she met Trinny, Susannah was known to venture outside in spotted jackets and velvet hair bands. Big loop earrings were her constant companions and she was not averse to a spot of tartan taffeta in the evenings.

She's never really been daring enough to go out on a limb with her own personal style. Her body has been the gateway to looking good, but since she has had a baby it's not just a question of slinging on anything and appearing passable. This has been a difficult habit to break, as she is an intrinsically lazy dresser who is quite happy to wear the same jeans all week. Trinny, however, is teaching her to be more concerned with her looks. Fuss and frills have been abandoned in place of simple cuts that are still feminine and sexy.

HOW SUSANNAH SEES HERSELF

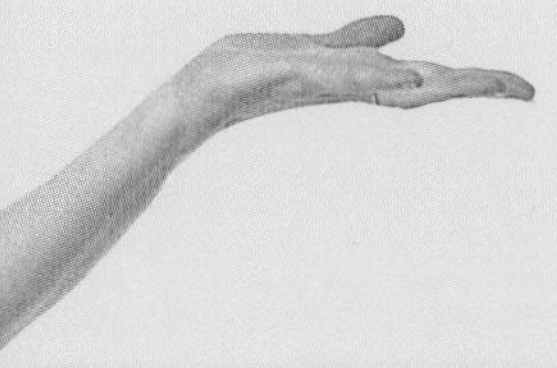

• Flying flab swings from my upper arms
• A stomach softer and with more movement than a waterbed
• The broken vein on my nose makes me look like I've walked into a wall
• My mammoth mammaries make me look fat...
• ...and baggy knees don't help

HOW TRINNY SEES SUSANNAH

• Delicate wrists and fine fingers
• A belly with its own life, but nothing a few sit-ups wouldn't improve
• Glorious skin that glows even after a heavy night
• A great pair of tits, which are famous for their firmness
• Gorgeous long legs that I want to carve off and fuse to my hips

SUSANNAH

Worst looks

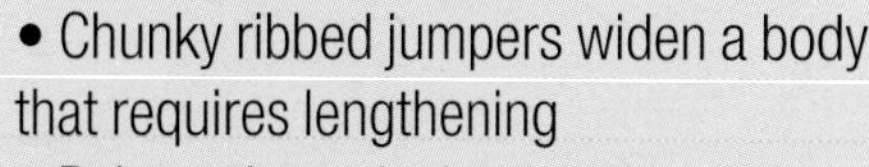

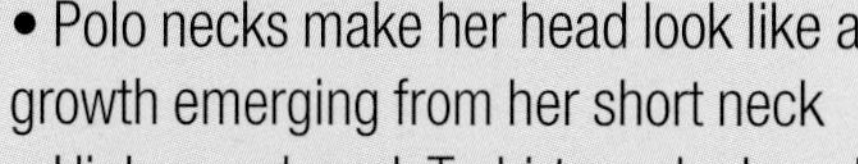

- Chunky ribbed jumpers widen a body that requires lengthening
- Polo necks make her head look like a growth emerging from her short neck
- High round-neck T-shirts make her chest look like a continuation of her chin
- Capped sleeves on big arms look like baby berets on a mountain of flesh
- Double-breasted anything

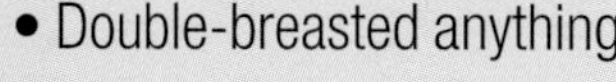

Best looks

- Tight dresses with a low neckline and fitted waist accentuate all those curves
- Deep V-neck jumpers, low round-neck T-shirts, round-neck cardigans undone at the top – all show that stunning cleavage
- Three-quarter length sleeves, to hide the flab at the top, but display delicate wrists
- Wrap tops pull tits forward and spotlight waist
- Bias-cut skirts to the calf cling to shapely legs
- Pencil skirts to the knee cling to pert bum and slender thighs for a lecherous look

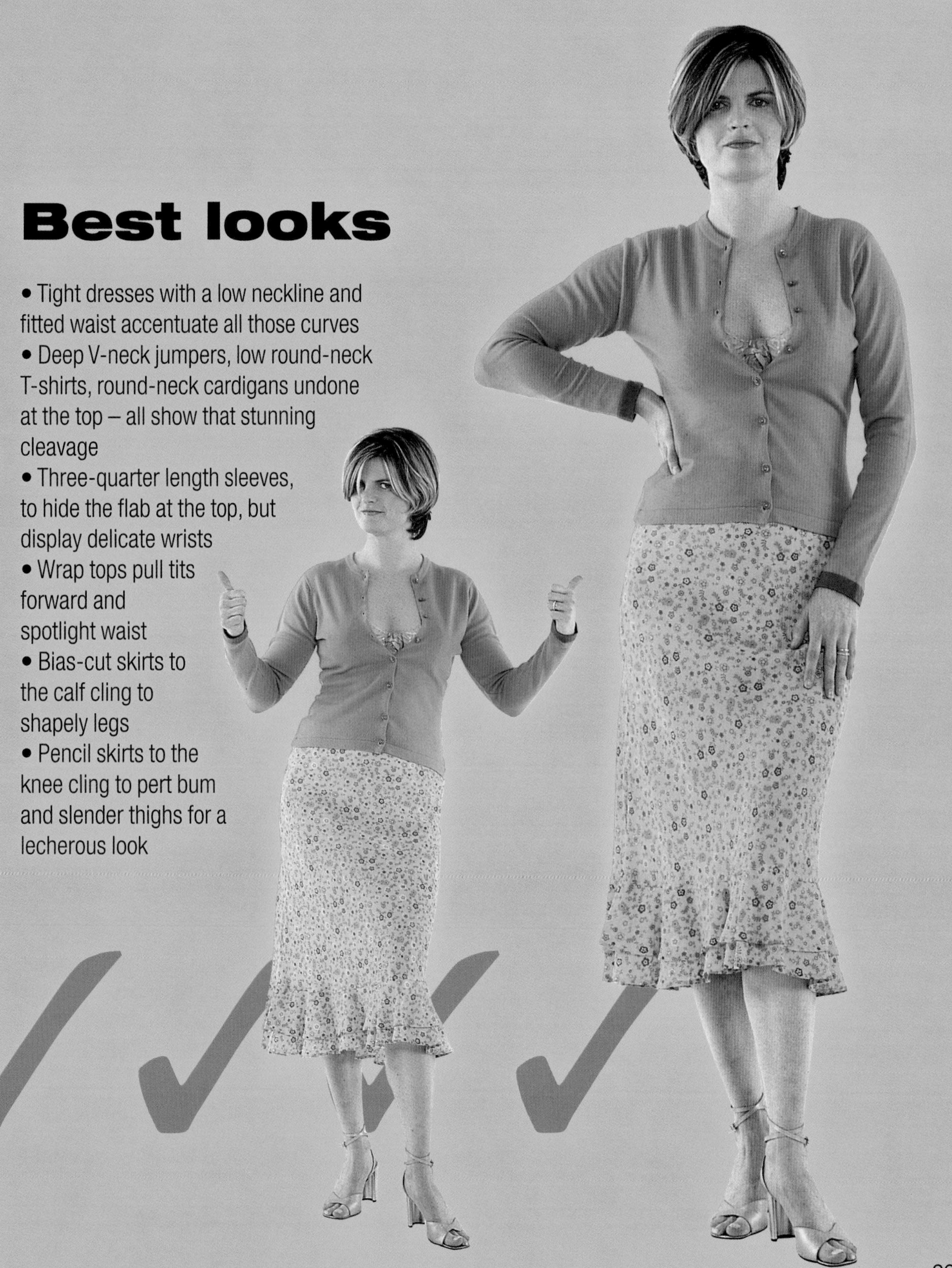

JOANNA

wasp-waisted bell bum

Joanna is pushing 40 and engrossed in a successful career, which would be discarded in a flash for the right man. She lives alone in a small but exquisitely designed home. She is everyone's best friend because of her rabid enthusiasm for partying. As long as she remains single, she will cling to the habits – and hairstyle – of her youth. Yet just because she is stuck in her ways does not mean she is devoid of insecurities – like feeling over the hill and not sexy – and her small, sloping shoulders can make her appear unconfident. There is always something slightly wrong with her dress sense. This may be a heel just too high for a country walk, or a sanitary towel just too bulky for her overly tight retro jeans.

She is a classic pear. Though she takes great care of herself and frequents the gym with religious fervour, her wide ass doesn't seem to benefit from repeated bum lifts and her saddlebags never empty.

HOW SHE SEES HERSELF

• If I stop working out, I feel I'll end up like my mother
• I think my hair is my one asset
• My shoulders are so sloping, I feel my cheeks are going to landslide down the side of them
• I would love to have a defined jaw line
• My bum blocks out the sun
• If I had a chest, I know I'd be happier

HOW WE SEE HER

• A stunningly toned body that is aged by the way she dresses
• If she had the courage to cut her hair it would take years off her
• Who cares about shoulders? Isn't that what shoulder pads are for? (Use only in moderation)
• Amazing bone structure which holds together a skin worn by hard living
• Bursting buttocks make her tiny waist look minute
• No tits? Slip in fake ones

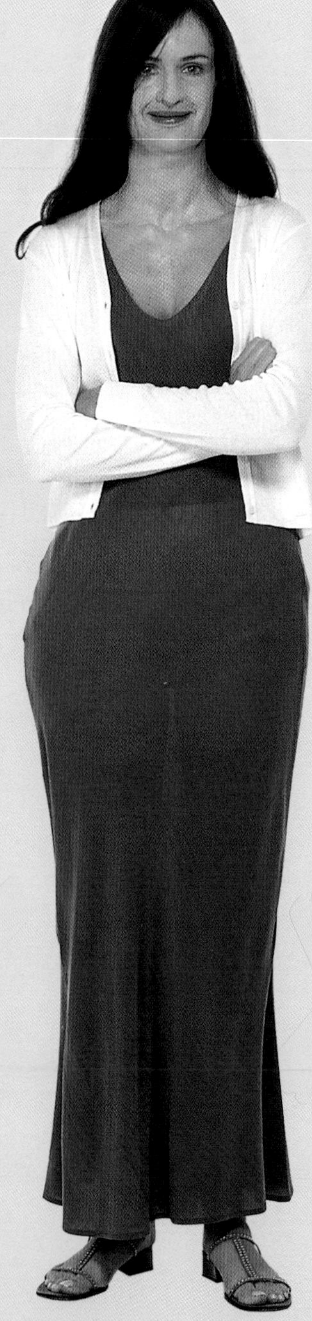

JOANNA

Worst looks

- Tight cocktail dresses: if it fits on her bum, it won't fit anywhere else
- Trousers with pleats will be pulled out by fat backside
- Delicate tops accentuate her pathetic shoulders
- Thick chunky chokers strangle her
- Long dresses cut on the bias will make her bum look like a lollipop on a stick

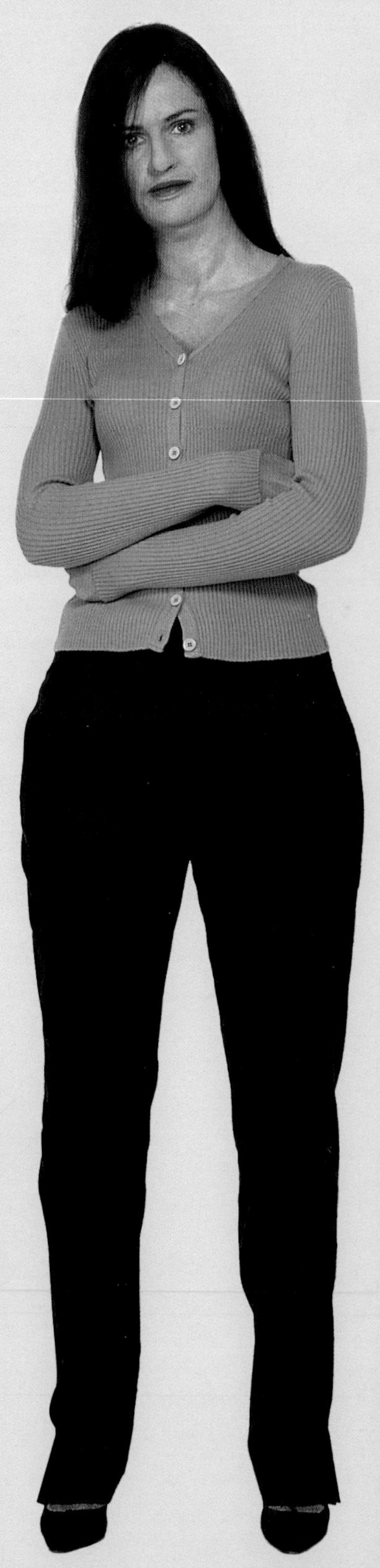

Best looks

- Trouser suits with long-line jackets to cover difference between ass and shoulders
- Shirt collars and scarves to give neck some credibility
- Shoulder pads to disguise her lack of shoulder width and balance her girth
- Pencil skirts to hold everything in
- Thank heavens for the A-line skirt – tailor-made for broad beams

ROSEMARY

big-bellied turkey neck

Stylish in her 20s and 30s, but by the time she reached 60 she had traded in any individuality she once had for the sake of fitting in with her bridge-playing friends. She shops at M & S and wherever else her friends go. Her waist went with the advent of M & S prepacked convenience foods and her boobs now fall like Niagara, so she tends to stick to tents and baggy separates.

She is desperate to break out of the mould and let her individual flair have a second chance. What prevents her is the fear of looking like Mrs Doubtfire on E. She is a bit of a drinker, which accounts for her rather florid complexion. Her hair is as grey and hard as granite thanks to a set that hasn't changed in 20 years. She is quite set in her ways and hard to approach with criticism.

HOW SHE SEES HERSELF

• I feel a little beyond my sell-by date – especially as the HRT hasn't kicked in yet
• There is no definition between my knee and my calf
• I am surprised more people don't want to wring my neck, it's so scrawny
• My stomach is bigger than my breasts
• My backside has melted down the backs of my legs

HOW WE SEE HER

• She is a very graceful, serene-looking woman
• Are you considering wearing miniskirts?
• At least her neck is long enough to take the kind of thing it should be hidden behind – like chokers and polo necks
• Her tummy is well rounded, but she doesn't need to wear things that make her look like a pot-bellied pig
• At least her bum is flat!

ROSEMARY

Worst looks

- Front-zipped trousers will enhance her eternally 'pregnant' stomach
- Pleat-fronted trousers will do the same
- Tight leggings make her look like a marathon runner who would never make the finish
- Anything with a low neckline will make her feel old whenever she looks in the mirror
- Floaty dresses that let it all hang out – it's such an aging look

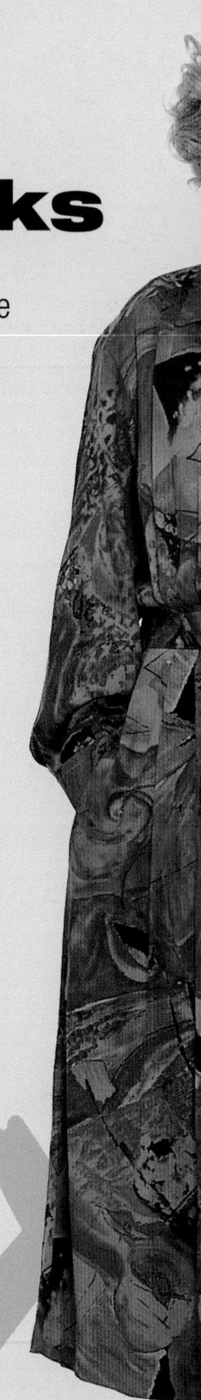

Best looks

- Chokers and polo necks – to hide her crepy neck
- Bootleg trousers which skim the top of the calf and cover the thickening ankle
- Jersey tied around the waist for a youthful edge
- Long-line tunic tops – to slim her down, elongate her shape and hide her bulge
- Tailored dresses to hold it all in
- A smoother, sleeker hairstyle knocks ten years off her age

SUMMARY

Now that we and our four friends have lain ourselves bare, it's up to you to do the same. We don't for one minute assume that you will identify entirely with one person, but feel sure that you will share horrors and assets with each of them. If you have the legs of Susannah, bust of Normandy and waist of Joanna, lucky you. If, however, your stomach is like Rosemary's, tits like Trinny's and thighs like Lorna's, life must be pretty diabolical. But don't despair.

Given the best and even the worst scenarios, there will always be ways you can improve your image through clever dressing. It's a matter of deciding which bits you want to flaunt and which you need to flatter. So if you are an ideal woman, be humble; and if you are elephant woman, take heart.

To look fabulous you don't need to go to the gym or diet your eyeballs out. It's just a case of covering the lumps and bumps. Once you realize style is not about fashion, it's about what suits you, you will gain the confidence and knowledge to shop for new clothes. Taking the plunge and being true to your physical make-up will mean you'll look different from your friends. Get them to read this book too!

THE TEN COMMANDMENTS

1. Get naked in front of the mirror to evaluate what you love and hate about yourself. Don't forget to check the rear view.
2. Put on an outfit you never end up wearing. Ask yourself exactly why is it not flattering.
3. Put on the outfit you feel most confident in and work out why you like it so much. What does it cover and what does it reveal?
4. Do you feel you are letting yourself go? Ask yourself why.
5. Re-assess your hairstyle. Has it been the same for many years? It may be safe but perhaps it's time for a change.
6. Write a list of things you don't like about yourself. Then write down how you can disguise them.
7. Write a list of your assets and how you can show them to best advantage.
8. Ask your most stylish friend to 'mark' your lists.
9. Chuck out the clothes that don't suit you – even if you think of them as old friends.
10. Gather up your lists and go shopping – but you might like to read the rest of this book first!

2

THE BARE ESSENTIALS

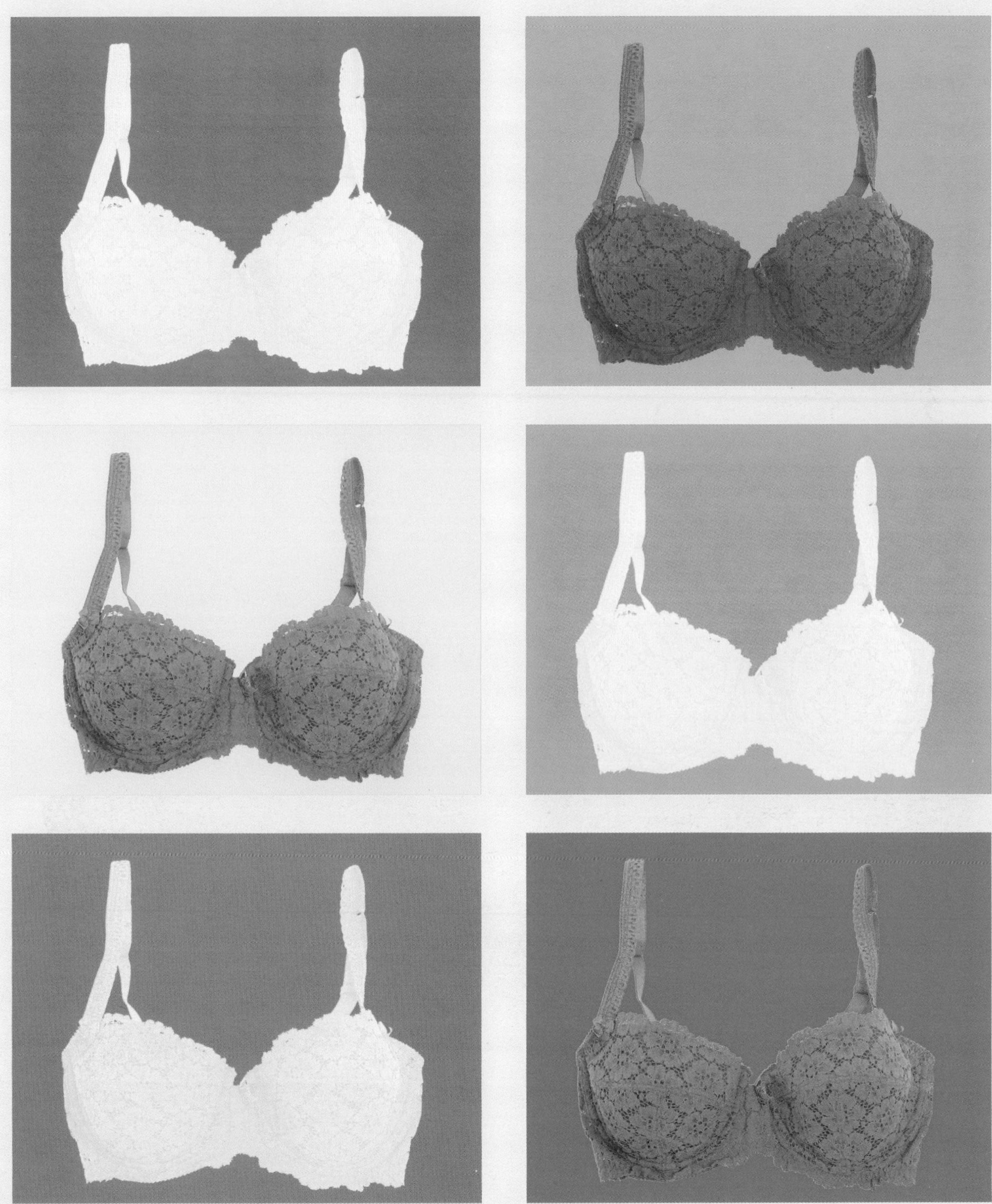

INTRODUCTION

Having deconstructed all female physical defects and ascertained the assets, it's time now to lay bare the essentials every girl needs in her wardrobe. At first, you will no doubt glance over the ensuing items and delight in the fact that your shelves and rails are packed with all of them. Ah, but are they the right shape for you?

It's all well and good having an abundance of jackets, but if some are double-breasted and God gave you mountainous mammaries, the parallel rows of buttons will double your size.

This explains why you testily discard them on a pile of equally ill-chosen clothes each time you attempt to wear them. Unfortunately, even a garment in your best colour will never feel right if it doesn't suit your shape. This is why so many of us take hours to get ready. It's not a lack of clothes that makes dressing such a trial, but more a shortage of the bare necessities that really work for you.

Once you have determined the style of key items that conceal your defects and exhibit your assets, you can use them as the basis for everyday dressing upon which to build your individual style. And hey, getting ready for any occasion will become effortless and a whole lot more fun.

Suits you,
Susannah
Absolutely
fabulous, Trinny

T-SHIRTS

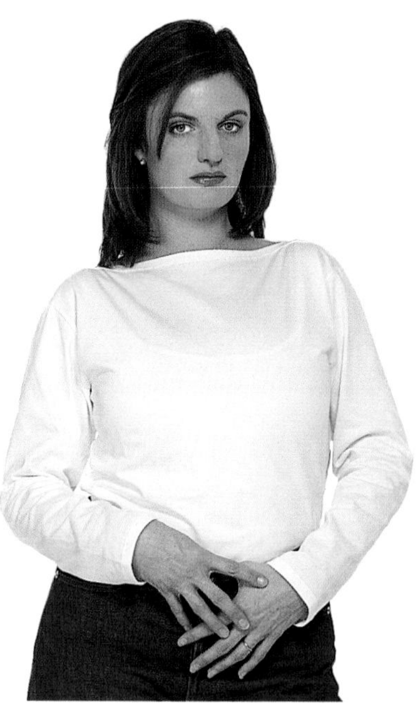

NORMANDY

Best type: V-neck vest
Why: shows off her slim arms, while the low V-neck breaks up her chest and prevents her tits looking like they are an extension of her chin

Worst type: capped sleeved slash neck
Why: makes her arms look like spindles and tits like balloons semi-filled with water

LORNA

Best type: long sleeved slash neck
Why: stylish, and covers without clinging

Worst type: anything clinging
Why: rolls of fat will wobble like an elaborate jelly

TRINNY

Best type: sleeveless, high round neck, long waisted
Why: shows off the arms she loves, while its length prevents an elongating space appearing between the T-shirt and a skirt or trousers

Worst type: cropped with a deep V-neck
Why: does everything to expose a barren chest and nothing to shorten her very long back

SUSANNAH

Best type: tight sleeves and a low round neck

Why: sleeve ends at the thinnest part of her bulbous upper arm and soft low neckline breaks up chest area and compliments her curvaceous figure

Worst type: high round neck with no sleeves

Why: arms are the unbecoming focal point – competing rather too closely with boobs

JOANNA

Best type: cropped T-shirt with a high round neck

Why: the eye is drawn to her pleasingly small waist and the high neck creates a more angled jaw line

Worst type: long, loose T-shirt

Why: ends at her hips and hides her best asset, her waist

ROSEMARY

Best type: long, loose cotton jersey tunic – and sleeves cover the upper arm, which ages first

Why: she's got to cover that tummy with a top that doesn't cling to it and she'll need a neat scarf to conceal her crepy gullet

Worst type: being older she shouldn't wear T-shirts – especially clinging, deep V-necked styles with short sleeves

Why: wrinkle city. How undignified

TOPS

NORMANDY

Best type: skinny rib polo neck (worn with right bra to lift and separate)
Why: accentuates her breasts without being vulgar

Worst type: unfitted, sleeveless shell top
Why: udders take on a lumpy quality like badly made custard and her arms resemble pretzel sticks

LORNA

Best type: wrap-around shirt
Why: holds it all together and the deep wrap makes her neck look longer and shoulders less like Hulk Hogan's

Worst type: halter neck
Why: shows off the whopping shoulders, while the low back means she can't wear a bra. The result? Two teats prone to truancy at the cut-away sides

TRINNY

Best type: round halter-neck
Why: shows off her best features: her back and arms. It's the one garment where no boobs are an advantage

Worst type: deep V-neck in shiny fabric
Why: accentuates boniness, while shiny fabric intensifies the disadvantage her petite top has over the larger lower half of her body

SUSANNAH

Best type: tight, suck-it-all-in T-shirt (preferably with a built-in bra) with three-quarter length sleeves
Why: a tight fit shows her super-glued body to perfection (in-built bra gives double security), the sleeves hide those leg-o'-mutton arms

Worst type: camisole top
Why: far too delicate for such an erupting torso

JOANNA

Best type: cropped, round neck or ballerina top, tied at the side
Why: tops that end around her waist emphasize its tininess, so long as the flesh of her flat tum is on display

Worst type: long-line cardigan
Why: hemline stretched to the limit over her Titanic hips

ROSEMARY

Best type: high neck tunic-style shirt, possibly with attached cravat tie (only in the best silk) or worn with a long-line waistcoat
Why: got to cover this neck with elegance; a cravat emphasizes its length. Long waistcoat keeps her streamlined

Worst type: deep V-neck in stretchy, synthetic fabric
Why: neck and décolleté have to be covered, while stretchy fabric broadcasts tum

TROUSERS

NORMANDY

Best type: hipster bootleg
Why: hipster gives her a waist and bootleg balances tits

Worst type: tight straight leg
Why: make her look even more top heavy and accentuate the fact that she has no ass

LORNA

Best type: hipsters with loose straight legs
Why: those misshapen legs look long and lithe

Worst type: any trousers with side pockets
Why: side pockets add width to injury, making her look like a stunted dwarf

TRINNY

Best type: hipsters with side zip and straight legs
Why: hipster waistline minimizes length of back. Straight leg doesn't cling to low ass or thick calf

Worst type: tight, high waisted drainpipe
Why: accentuate low bum and will not fit around waist, leaving unattractive gape

SUSANNAH

Best type: waisted, flat-fronted with side zip, narrow straight legs
Why: accentuate length of legs and hold in tummy with no fuss at the front to bulk it up

Worst type: wide, short legged
Why: best feature looks stunted. Little ankles look like worms coming out of Channel tunnel

JOANNA

Best type: side fastening palazzo pants
Why: wide-bottomed trousers make her pear bum look more in proportion with her slight top half

Worst type: high-waisted trousers
Why: her waist – one of her best features – becomes redundant

ROSEMARY

Best type: palazzo pants in jersey
Why: she needs to hide her tree-trunk legs and her trousers cannot be too tight or they will emphasize her rotund belly

Worst type: front-zipped straight leg, jean cut
Why: that zip is a beacon to her tummy

SKIRTS

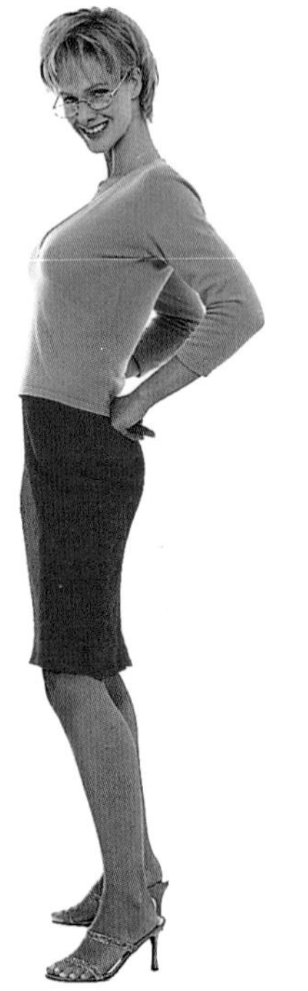

NORMANDY

Best type: structured A-line to just above the knee
Why: A-line balances out her tits and gives substance to her lack of hip and ass

Worst type: long, floaty fabric, elasticized waist
Why: swamps her, covering up her bottom half and leaving only her tits on view

LORNA

Best type: stretch-waisted, worn low and long
Why: lack of structure around waist allows for skimming down the silhouette

Worst type: A-line above the knee
Why: shows off fatty knees and shortens silhouette

TRINNY

Best type: A-line to the knee
Why: ends at narrowest part of upper leg, elongating lower leg; skims over bottom without accentuating it

Worst type: calf length, cut on bias
Why: stunts legs and thickens calves even further, broadens by clinging to worst areas

SUSANNAH
Best type: below the knee, bell shape pencil skirt
Why: covers baggy knees, clings to the leg (her best part) and accentuates the elegance of her shape by showing off her good calves. Also shows off the sexy curve of her ass

Worst type: short A-line
Why: knees look knobbly

JOANNA
Best type: sarong skirt
Why: winches in waist and the folds of fabric soften the contrast between her hips and waist

Worst type: any skirt cut on the bias
Why: her ass will take on its own life

ROSEMARY
Best type: below the knee, wherever she can find a narrow part. Tapered and plain
Why: the skirt must do nothing to attract the eye to the legs, so the plainer the better: never patterned, floaty or clingy

Worst type: gathered at the waist, calf-length, in bright colour
Why: makes her belly even bigger

JACKETS

NORMANDY

Best type: very fitted, very deep V, cut to hip
Why: lengthens the torso by the cut; the deep V divides the tits

Worst type: boxy, short-waisted jacket
Why: makes her bottom half look anorexic

LORNA

Best type: three-quarter length, single-breasted, round neck, no collar
Why: elongates her shape, hides the pear, makes her shortish neck more elegant

Worst type: any short jacket
Why: displays pear shape

TRINNY

Best type: long-line, single-breasted, tight fitting. Narrow but long lapel
Why: long line covers ass, deceives eye on leg length. Lapel elongates narrow body, accentuating slimness

Worst type: short-waisted fitted jacket
Why: shows off short legs and long waist

SUSANNAH
Best type: short-waisted, tight fitting, single-breasted, small lapel
Why: accentuates long legs, small lapel narrows shoulder

Worst type: long-line Nehru jacket
Why: makes short neck disappear and tits look insignificant, leaving no room for a curvaceous sexy shape

JOANNA
Best type: single-breasted, waisted, covering bum
Why: skims over big bum

Worst type: straight blazer
Why: hides her waist and clings around her bum

ROSEMARY
Best type: long and staight with narrow shoulders
Why: skims rather than clings, while small shoulders make her look less weighed down by life

Worst type: belted jacket
Why: how is it going to do up?

DRESSES

NORMANDY

Best type: low neck, below the knee
Why: emphasizes her feminine shape

Worst type: deep V-neck with spangly bits
Why: brings vulgarity to her style

LORNA

Best type: off the shoulder with long, flowing skirt
Why: soft, feminine and subtly sexy

Worst type: wide-strapped A-line with small round neck
Why: accentuates all big points of body and covers up good bits

TRINNY

Best type: high, round halter neck, to the knee, tight at top not at bottom
Why: shows off arms, hits legs at thinnest part

Worst type: bias-cut, V-neck, short-sleeved, ending mid calf
Why: turns her into a total pear shape

SUSANNAH

Best type: sweetheart neckline, puff sleeves, empire line
Why: hides tummy, shows off legs, gathered fabric prevents tit-clinging

Worst type: spaghetti strap slip
Why: thinness of straps enhances size of shoulders, arms and tits

JOANNA

Best type: sleeveless, deep V-neck; could be ankle-length
Why: deep V draws the eye to décolleté and hence away from the hips

Worst type: round neck shirtdress
Why: the size she would need for her hips would lose her nipped-in waist

ROSEMARY

Best type: coat dress – woolly or light
Why: shows good shoulders, hides tummy

Worst type: empire line tent dress
Why: she feels it hides the tummy but in fact it makes her appear far bigger than she is

COATS

NORMANDY

Best type: narrow, deep V-neck and small lapel; or swing coat
Why: evens out her irregular shape. Swing coat reverses her triangle shape

Worst type: belted
Why: makes everything up top too bulky

LORNA

Best type: classic crombie
Why: makes her the same shape all the way down rather than bigger around the hips

Worst type: short double-breasted coat
Why: makes her square

TRINNY

Best type: narrow, long-line, one-button crombie
Why: slim line follows shape of body. Position of button elongates legs

Worst type: double-breasted, with princess collar
Why: gives no waist definition

SUSANNAH

Best type: waisted, with small lapel
Why: good deep V does not constrict tits. Nipped-in waist shows curvaceous figure

Worst type: classic crombie
Why: covers up all best features

JOANNA

Best type: slim-line, single-breasted, with princess collar
Why: unfussy top half looks neat, skims ass

Worst type: belted raincoat
Why: flares out at hips, accentuating them

ROSEMARY

Best type: well cut and gently tailored, to the calf
Why: very elegant, hides tummy

Worst type: belted raincoat
Why: the belt will slide up to below her chest, prompting people to wonder when the baby is due

SHOES

NORMANDY

Best type: high heel, open toe, with strap across foot at angle
Why: strap at angle doesn't cut off the length of leg

Worst type: ballerina slippers
Why: have you ever seen a prima ballerina with big tits?

LORNA

Best type: low kitten heels
Why: she has good ankles but anything too high would make her appear top heavy

Worst type: dainty stilettoes
Why: just a matter of time before her weight snaps the heel

TRINNY

Best type: high court with strap across foot
Why: height makes legs look longer and strap draws focus away from porky ankle

Worst type: flat ballerina pumps
Why: not substantial enough to take on her thick ankle

SUSANNAH

Best type: elegant high slingback with narrow heel
Why: like a continuation of her elegant ankle

Worst type: chunky loafers
Why: her foot resembles that of a clown in a big shoe

JOANNA

Best type: round-toed court shoe with thick heel
Why: it's sturdy enough to take the ass and high enough to give her elegance

Worst type: kitten heels
Why: will make her appear top heavy

ROSEMARY

Best type: narrow, low wedge, or pointed slingback with thicker heel
Why: wedge or thick heel help balance tree trunks; pointed slingback gives definition to legs

Worst type: high-heeled round-toed court shoes
Why: make her ankles look like stumps because the back of the shoe cut them off

T-shirt or
not T-shirt…

...that is the question.

SUMMARY

Now you have the foundation for an eclectic wardrobe, making it individual and truly representative of your personality will be the next phase. Using the basics as a yardstick you can begin buying the relevant shapes in colours and fabrics that suit you. At the risk of stating the obvious, thick, highly textured, shiny and clingy fabrics will accentuate bodily features, as will big patterns. Don't be frightened of colour, just make sure it's accentuating your bon points. Armed with this knowledge, the massive choice available on the high street will be refined as your trained eye edits out the clothes you shouldn't go near.

THE TEN COMMANDMENTS

1. Fat arms must always wear sleeves.
2. Big tits must only wear low neck T-shirts; flat chests need high necklines.
3. Big tummies must never wear hipsters.
4. Big bums must never wear jackets that end at the ass.
5. Saddlebags must never wear cut-on-the-bias skirts or dresses.
6. Thick calves must never wear three-quarter length dresses or skirts.
7. Baggy knees should always be covered.
8. Thick ankles must never wear delicate strappy high heels.
9. Leggings are for the gym and nowhere else.
10. Use shiny fabrics and bright colours only to draw attention to parts that can take it.

GETTING IT WRONG AND HOW TO GET IT RIGHT

INTRODUCTION

It is quite amazing how a woman can go out and spend a fortune on a fabulous outfit, only to ruin it with the wrong shoes. She may well be right in thinking that the black satin slingbacks have always looked divine with her charcoal skirt, but to wear them with a light, wispy chiffon is pure madness. We have lost count of the times our heads have swivelled admiringly at a stunningly dressed lady, looked her up and down and been flabbergasted by her choice of footwear.

Likewise with jewellery. There are occasions when a mass of pearls can work wonders for a simple dress, but do the same with gold and you commit style suicide. People won't believe you are any more prosperous if you put on your entire jewellery box. In this case less is more.

Many screaming faux pas are not obvious to the untrained eye. It could merely be a lace trim that's too bulky on a bra or, more seriously, a knicker line that's giving you four cheeks instead of two. It is these kind of peeping misdemeanours that prevent you from having style.

Twinkle, twinkle, it's so simple...when you know how

Now you *can* go to the ball

UNDERWEAR

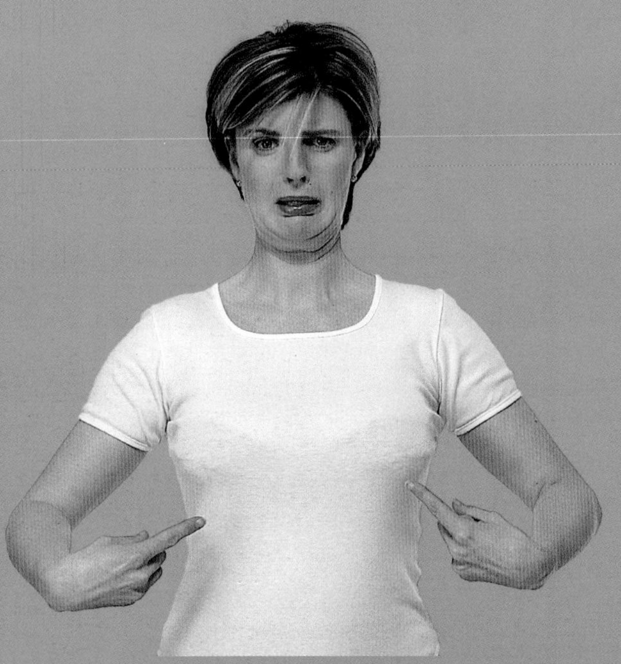

• No matter how cold or how desperate, tights under trousers are a disaster. They act like a magnet, making the fabric cling unattractively. The result is thighs that appear twice their size.
• Just because tights aren't laddered doesn't mean they are okay to wear. Snags are trashy, too.
• Don't be afraid to display bra straps under spaghetti strap dresses – but make sure they are pretty.

DON'T

• Never put on underwear that's darker than the clothes you are wearing.
• Bras and knickers should never be too tight, so check front, side and rear views in a mirror.
• Don't be fooled into thinking that the tighter a support knicker the better it will work. All that happens is your stomach will squidge up and over the waistband, giving a bizarrely high beer belly.
• No knickers and getting a crusty gusset is better than a visible panty line.
• Tights above 20 denier should only be in black.
• If you are going to show off your legs later, don't wear pop socks, as they inevitably leave ugly, smarting indentations.

• Wear body-controlling underwear when the contour of cellulite shows through lightweight fabric.
• All legs like to be longer, so wear socks or pop socks in the same colour as your trousers and give the illusion that your legs are at least 2 inches longer.
• Fold your Wonderbra cups in half and tuck them under tiny tits to push them up and closer for an exaggerated cleavage.
• Have your bust size professionally measured, as the chances are your bra is the wrong size.

DO

• Always wear a flesh-coloured bra with a white T-shirt.
• If any garment is even the tiniest bit see through, be certain to wear flesh-coloured undies.
• If a skirt is see through but not clingy, flesh-coloured granny knickers work better than a G-string.
• Wear a G-string with tight trousers. If you don't have a clean one make do with a tampon.
• Check your G-string matches your flesh tone. If it's darker people will assume loo paper is not a feature in your home.

HANDBAGS

DON'T

- Don't carry a summery basket when wearing a tailored suit.
- Don't wear heavy leather bags with summer clothing.
- Don't wear a structured bag with unstructured clothing.
- Don't carry a wicker basket when you are wearing tights or they will snag.
- Don't wear a beaded bag with a beaded dress – choose a satin bag.
- Don't be tempted to buy the handbag of the season if it breaks the bank; the high street always copies bags well.

Coloured outfit with brown bag

Evening dress with day bag

DO

- Make sure your bag is of the same ilk as your shoes – it needn't match exactly but must have something in common.
- Make sure your bags are in proportion to your size.
- Wear beaded bags with plain velvet; don't wear velvet with velvet.
- Go to markets to find individual or antique bags that will make a good talking point at a party.
- Keep bags that you are not using covered to protect them from dust.
- If possible, hang up evening bags with your jewellery, so you see them and use them more often.

Coloured outfit with co-ordinating bag

Evening dress with pretty bag

JEWELLERY

DON'T

• Don't wear a big choker if you have a short neck.
• Don't wear quantities of gold jewellery at the same time.
• Don't wear long pendants if you have big tits.
• Don't wear big round earrings if you have short hair – they will dominate your face.
• Don't turn down eccentric baubles from a mad aunt – in a few years you may appreciate them for the same reasons she did.

Too much gold

Engulfed neck

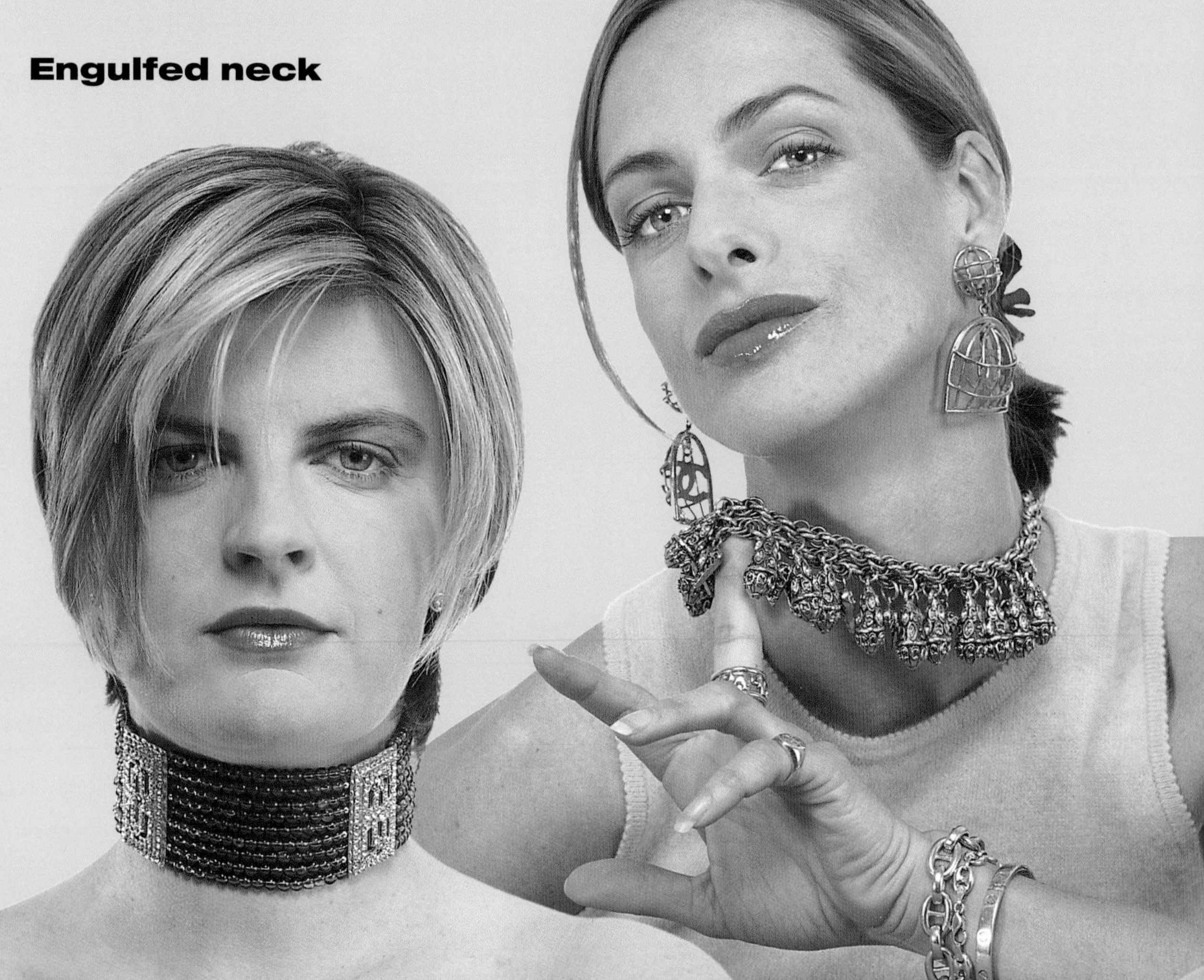

DO

- Remember too little is better than too much.
- If you have got a double chin, longer earrings will be more flattering.
- Go into teenage type stores for fun summer jewellery at a fraction of the cost of designer versions.
- Look for unusual antique jewellery to enhance your individual style.

Subtle gold

Delicate choker

SHOES

DON'T

- Never wear court shoes without tights.
- Don't wear black shoes with light coloured clothing – unless they are very dainty sandals.
- Don't ever wear wedge trainers – you might think they make your legs look longer, but it's at a cost to your ankles, which will look even thicker.
- Don't wear trainers with white socks unless you are at the gym or playing tennis.
- Never wear flesh-coloured tights with sandals – but do paint your toenails.
- Never have a high heel on full display at the end of jeans – it will make the jeans look too short.
- Never wear tapered leg trousers with court shoes or boots – wear flat, chunky-soled shoes.

Delicate skirt and dark shoes

Jeans and high heels

DO

- Wear only flat shoes or boots with jeans.
- Wear shoes and socks in the same colour as trousers.
- Wear only wedge or flat shoes with short wide trousers.
- With mid calf pencil skirts only wear high heels.
- With bias-cut long skirts only wear flats, kitten mules, or boots.
- Hosiery and socks should be plain – never patterned.
- If you are top-heavy, don't highlight heftiness by wearing delicate shoes with a short skirt length.

Pale shoes with delicate outfit

Flat sandals with jeans

SUMMARY

It's too late to cry over embarrassments of the past. Yes, we've all walked out of public loos with our skirt tucked in our knickers, but there's no point in dwelling on unfortunate accidents. We've all worn dodgy bras and clumpy shoes with delicate dresses. Most of us, however, have no idea that these are, in fact, serious style errors, so how can we learn from our mistakes? No one is immune: Susannah still insists on granny knickers when the panty line might be visible, albeit only just, and Trinny continues to forget about the etiquette of bra wearing, and will wander out with her nipples demanding attention. If you have a friend who commits these blunders, tell them. We do.

THE TEN COMMANDMENTS

1. Don't ever leave the house without doing the bra test. If you can see the contours of padding or lace, take it off.
2. Any panty line on the rear is revolting.
3. Never, ever wear white shoes with dark or autumn/winter outfits.
4. Black and brown shoes should never be worn with pale outfits.
5. High-heeled shoes and jeans are to be avoided at all costs.
6. Leather bags prefer the winter unless pale or brightly coloured.
7. Leather bags should never be worn in the evening – not even tiny weeny ones.
8. The only time you can get away with a lot of gold is when it's in your mouth.
9. Short necks that hold a small head must never wear thick necklaces.
10. Thick hair bands and large earrings have never worked and nor will they ever.

4

BASIC BEAUTY

Ready 2 Kiss?

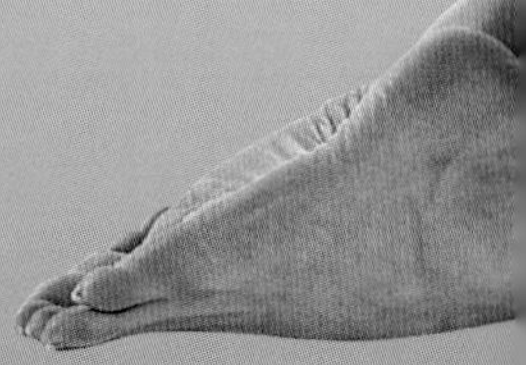

I didn't know you cared
Help!… Let me out of here!

INTRODUCTION

Believe it or not, there are women who aren't thrown by the sudden arrival of a zit. These are not the supermodels, who make a career from flawless features. Nor are they the heroines of the big screen. The Kims and Meryls are more neurotic than anyone about physical perfection. Women who are at peace with their defects are those who are too busy or too powerful to care – and those who have learnt to camouflage the problem and move on with their lives.

Before we launch into a chapter dedicated to solving cosmetic crises, it's important to understand that our advice is based on our own experience rather than medical know-how. We don't pretend to be experts, but in our job we encounter beauty problems and solutions every day – cosmetic products are sent to us by the bathroom-load. This gives us plenty of opportunity to test, approve the ones we love and dispose of those we hate. Not that the answer always lies in a beauty product. Sometimes it's as simple as applying ketchup to discoloured highlights or wearing surgical gloves to massage in fake tan.

We also know all about chasing the impossible dream to achieve an impeccable physique. You can certainly focus your exercise routine to firm up the wobbly bits, but (almost) no one is perfect. Only the very young and bodily blessed have never felt horror at the thought of exposing a cellulite-laden thigh or fat bum to the unsuspecting world.

For those who believe worrying about blemishes and boils is for the vain and superficially driven, think again. Acne can ruin lives. It can result in never going out for fear that people will address the spots rather than the person. Likewise cellulite can prevent women ever wearing a bikini on the beach.

Take heart, O vulnerable ones, because nothing is insurmountable. We appreciate that all is relative, but letting a beauty problem take control of your life to the extent where you are ruled by it is not healthy.

We hope our home-spun discoveries and more radical suggestions help, because we sympathize with the amount of shit a little old pimple can dump on your day.

HAIR

There is no escaping the fact that a girl's hair is her crowning glory. A woman can be shoulder-to-toe gorgeousness, but if her hair is in any way out of sorts it will cause her image to slide every time. We aren't saying that you have to have that salon-fresh look on a daily basis, but a sleek professional blow-dry does wonders for special occasions and is well worth the money.

Before helping Lorna and Joanna turn themselves into effortlessly stylish women it was necessary to address their hair. One needed to go back to her roots and the other to get over her scissor phobia.

LORNA

Lorna has had the same hairstyle since she reached puberty. In her teens it was the envy of all her friends, whose mums wouldn't let them near a pot of dye, let alone a perm. The condition of her hair is now so appalling that she assumes it is beyond help. As a result she keeps up the same old dye'n'perm routine that her hairdresser of the past 15 years should be castrated for allowing.

Why she hasn't changed it

- She hasn't had the time
- She doesn't have the confidence for a dramatic change
- She was known as a blond, blue-eyed beauty before she got married
- Her husband likes blondes

How it has helped her

- The change in colour immediately makes her hair look healthier
- The colour has lifted her complexion
- Her hair has been blown dry, taking out the frizziness and giving her a more sophisticated appearance
- All the straggly ends have been cut off
- Her husband fancies her even more – especially since his friends have started to give her the eye

JOANNA

Ever since she was a little girl, Joanna's hair has been commented on for its long, luscious thickness. Her mother insisted that her hairdresser only trim it, a tradition that continues to this day. In her teenage years she used it to shield her acne, but as it was permanently greasy this only exacerbated the problem. She is forever giving her frustrated hairdresser false starts like… 'Okay, time for the big chop,' then walking out with two inches off instead of one and a half. Once or twice she has ventured into a fringe, self-administered with a blunt razor. Like Samson, she is convinced her hair gives strength and security.

Why she hasn't changed it

- She believes it makes her look younger
- It's always complimented upon
- It's in great condition
- If it was short she couldn't put it up (but she never does anyway)
- Her acne has been replaced by scars
- Because of her aggressive business reputation, she feels it is one element that keeps her feminine and sexy

How it has helped her

- She looks five years younger
- She is able to wear many more styles of clothing
- She can do so much more with it than just tying it back
- Her skin has improved
- It doesn't drag her face down, her jaw line is more defined, her eyes look bigger
- By framing her face it is softer and more feminine
- She's got a new boyfriend

HINTS

- To disguise greasy hair during the day, put sunglasses on top of your head
- If your hair is very greasy and you don't have time to wash it before dinner, bung on some gel and smooth back into a ponytail
- For dandruff – smooth olive oil on to the scalp and leave for one hour. Remove by putting shampoo straight on to dry hair. Wash off and watch the dandruff disappear
- For dyed blond hair that goes green with chlorine – tomato ketchup will take away the discolouration. Apply and wash out like conditioner

SINS

- A perm of any description
- A tight blow-dry
- A set that is too rigid
- Too much hair spray
- Long hair over 45, unless it's swept up into a chic chignon
- Salt and pepper highlights
- Short hair with a hard middle parting

SPOTS

Spots for a teenager are the end of the world. To the individual, one pimple is as nightmarish as a face full, and acne can ruin lives. While the clear-skinned are snogging and flirting, the girl with zits is picking and popping. She craves dark dingy cafés and clubs and dreads elevators with neon lights that yell 'Hey, look at that girl's spots, they're so red!'

Trinny was one such girl. She suffered terribly as a youngster, to the point that her life was ruled by how many spots she had. During her first proper romance she would get up an hour early to reapply foundation in the hope that her boyfriend wouldn't notice the state of her skin. In moments of desperation she tried every specialized product on the market – Oxy, Clinique Clarifying Lotion 3 (toner/paint stripper) – as well as surgical spirit and toothpaste. All were slapped on in the hope that one might prove to be a miracle cure. Her only reprieve came during the summer holidays, when the sun dried up her spots. This interlude of clarity lasted three days before the sun cream had clogged her pores to breed more spots.

Fake tan is sometimes a temporary way out, but if spots are too mountainous the fake tan will give them their own orange auras. After ten tortured years Trinny fully understands the etiquette of spot maintenance, so here is her list of do's and don'ts.

SOLUTIONS

DON'T

- Don't pick
- Don't go to a restaurant with bright lighting on a hot date if the spots are in full bloom
- Don't sleep on the worst infected side: It doesn't let the spots breathe at night and wipes off any spot cream
- Don't over-camouflage with make-up: It only makes them more noticeable
- Don't use a cream cleanser
- Don't use very red lipstick when you have a beacon near your lips
- Don't talk about your spots – you will only draw attention to a problem most people haven't even noticed

DO

- Use toothpaste as emergency dry-out when no spot cream is available
- Use a PABA-free sunscreen
- Resort to antibiotics or alternative diets – spots are often a result of food sensitivities as well as hormone imbalances
- If you have a ripe spot that demands an emergency pop, remember the cardinal squeeze rule: you should see pus, blood and pus. The spot will come back unless you've got rid of the second bit of pus. And use fingertips, not nails

SHORT TERM

- Eve Lom Dynamite spot cream
- Toothpaste
- Concealer without too much oil, but not too drying (Laura Mercier Secret Camouflage and Trish McEvoy Concealer are fabulous)
- A concealer in the same colour as your foundation, applied before and after making up

MEDIUM TERM

- Try a change in diet – many acne sufferers have found that their skins have improved dramatically after cutting out dairy, wheat or yeast products
- Ask your doctor about antibiotics: they have worked for many long-term sufferers
- Stop picking and squeezing
- Change your beauty routine – no night creams, no cream cleansers

LONG TERM

- There are conflicting reports on Roaccutane. It is a steroid for which a prescription is required, and it is very expensive if you don't get it on the National Health. Although side effects include extremely dry lips and joints (exercise is not advised during its use), the results are visible within weeks. Spots start to dry out and the skin becomes thinner. Trinny found the long-term effects startlingly good. It must not be taken if you are going into the sun
- Retin-A has been prescribed for acne (it is also good for reducing wrinkles). Adverse effects include extreme sensitivity to the sun, resulting in pigmentation problems
- For those with acne scars, a number of cosmetic surgical treatments are available
- Laser is an alternative for deep scarring – there are a number of different types and a dermatologist will be able to advise the best treatment for the individual

SUN

As toddlers our diligent mums lathered us in sun block, but as soon as we were able to take control of that bottle, how many of us chucked it out in preference to the baby oil and tin foil method? Susannah grew out of this as she grew into chronic heat rash at the end of her teens, when holidays were spent in southern France. By contrast Trinny continued well into her 20s, and is blessed not have suffered the ravages too much sun can inflict on the skin. All that can be said is that she must have the hide of a dinosaur.

Nowadays we are far more aware of the long-term damage sunbathing can do. But however hard the fashion industry tries to promote the glories of an alabaster skin, don't tell us that even the porcelain-pale Nicole Kidman doesn't yearn for a gently golden body from time to time. We love the sun as much as we loathe the harmful effects – unquestionably, a tanned body does make one feel slimmer, healthier and better in summer clothes.

To get brown you have to be sensible and remember that too dark is vulgar and too pale a non-event. So how do you achieve the perfect compromise?

SOLUTIONS

SHORT TERM

Faking it is the only way to get an instant tan. We highly recommend St Tropez.

1. Take Body Shop Pumice Foot Scrub and rub well all over the body. Shower off dead cells to reveal the fresh skin underneath
2. Apply a moisturizer to areas you don't want to become too brown, such as knees, ankles and elbows. Cover your palms with moisturizer to prevent the tan staining your hands when applying or, better still, use disposable plastic surgical gloves
3. Apply the fake tan over one leg. Make sure you cover every part as St Tropez works by coverage rather than depth. Do not rub the lotion in too hard, or it will ball and come off
4. Wash your hands and reapply the moisturizer before you go on to the next leg. Repeat the handwashing before moving on to the torso
5. For a lighter, more natural facial tan, make sure that you moisturize well just before you apply fake tan to the face, unless you are going for the dried prune look
6. At this stage the St Tropez fake tan will look blotchy and streaky. Don't worry, this is normal
7. After ten minutes, when the lotion has dried, buff off the excess with a flannel
8. Go to bed
9. Wake up and take a shower to remove the excess. You should be left with a superb, even tan

MEDIUM/LONG TERM

When you go out in the sun, remember that the longer it takes you to build up your tan, the longer the tan will last. If you burn your tan won't last as long.

- On the first day make sure you apply a high factor sunscreen: 30 for the face and chest and 15 minimum for the rest of the body
- Gradually reduce the factor – except on your face and chest, where you will age a year every time you burn. There is nothing more aging than a crepy chest
- Throughout your holiday, keep applying fake tan to your face and chest to prevent the temptation of getting them the same colour as your body
- Exfoliate every evening to prevent peeling – don't forget to do your face
- You should return with a great, long-lasting tan

Prickly heat and sunburn

- Zirtek is a fab over-the-counter antihistamine. Start taking it a week before your holiday to prevent the itch of prickly heat
- If you burn, chilled live yogurt is wonderfully soothing
- Remember that hair burns too – but you can now buy specially formulated protective products
- You can burn through umbrellas, so keep applying the sunscreen

CELLULITE

The first time we encounter cellulite is as babies, but at that age, what do we care? There are then approximately 25 cellulite-free years when we look at orange-peel thighs first (as kids) with curiosity, then (as cocky teenagers) mockingly and then (as twenty-somethings) with pity. In our innocence we believe that cellulite will never happen to us. If only this was true. Like other physical dysfunctions it comes with age. Even the skinniest are not immune. For some women their breadcrumb bums and landscaped legs are so noticeable that they dare not venture out in a bikini unless covered from the waist down by a sarong. And covering cellulite does not always mean it's hidden. Tight leggings in any colour are not a foil. Nor are tight light summer trousers. They both display cellulite most efficiently.

Typically cellulite hits the upper thigh, but in older and post-baby women (like Susannah) it creeps up to the stomach, onto the arms and sometimes around to the back. Some women are not aware of just how bad and visible their cellulite is, while others complain of nothing else.

SHORT TERM SOLUTIONS

• Try the following:

1. Loofah the affected area hard and fast to get circulation pumping
2. Get into a warm bath and have a long soak
3. Leaving the warm water in the bath to take the edge off, use the shower attachment to spray the offending area with cold water for 30 seconds
4. Get out of the bath and apply Dior Svelte or Thalgo Marine Extract

• Have a wrap treatment. Some have a temporary reducing effect

MEDIUM TERM SOLUTIONS

• Change your diet. What you eat and drink affects cellulite, the worst enemies being: caffeine – and this includes tea; fizzy drinks – and this includes sparkling water; dairy products
• Work out – this prevents the fat from stagnating and breeding cellulite
• Give up smoking – all those toxins encourage the formation of cellulite

LONG TERM SOLUTIONS

• Liposuction – but the downside is that the fat will inevitably return to another part of the body
• Mesotherapy – injections full of vitamins and caffeine to get the cellulite shifting

HAIR REMOVAL

Anyone who believes that shaving is a sign of growing up exclusive to boys is quite wrong. How many of you girls started shaving non-existent leg hair with your dad's nicked razor because, like budding boobs, you thought sprouting body hair was a step closer to adulthood? Shaving meant it would grow back faster and grow it did. Faster, thicker and darker than you ever imagined.

Having to mow or wax one's legs is nothing compared to excess hair on the face. It's a bugger to get rid of and can ruin a beautiful girl. Shaving the upper lip is a disaster, as the rapid re-growth will give you a full-blown Sadam moustache within a week.

Shaving the pubes is an equally bad idea, resulting in unbecoming itching, and spots from ingrown hairs that make the knicker line look like it's been attacked by leeches. Launch a counter-attack by exfoliating and loofing every day – this will reduce ingrown hairs, especially around the pubic area.

Armpits must be kept hair-free by whatever means you choose – shaving is convenient and relatively painless. We believe that body odour is increased by allowing the jungle under your arms to run riot; although this pungent odour may turn on southern Mediterranean men, just remember that your fellow workers or tube passengers might not be so appreciative.

THE FACE

- Short term – bleaching
- Medium term – waxing
- Long term – electrolysis or laser treatment

PUBIC AREA

- Short term – wearing shorts instead of a bikini
- Medium term – waxing
- Long term – laser treatment or electrolysis (oh so painful)

LEGS AND UNDER ARMS

- Short term – shaving
- Medium term – waxing
- Long term – laser treatment (electrolysis takes too long for legs)

MAKE-UP

From a young age, a little girl is intuitively drawn to make-up. Her first foray as beautician is practised upon defenceless dolls and mute teddy bears. Using Sindy's own line of cosmetics, toys will be subjected to ham-fisted applications of eye shadow and lipstick. Unfortunately, many of these small girls continue to use the same slapdash methods well after they have grown up.

The shade of eye shadow favoured in toy make-up sets has always been bright, turquoise blue. This is a wonderful colour for a summer sky. The lipstick is invariably peachy orange. Sublime at sunset in the southern hemisphere. Blusher will either be sweetie red or chocolate brown. Good enough to eat and just as sickly.These cardinal colour combinations haven't really changed much over the years. Any girl who defined her make-up technique before the age of ten will undoubtedly be stuck in a cosmetic time warp and resemble a walking, talking, brightly made-up living doll.

The tomboys who felt more at home with Action Man than Barbie will have swung the other way. Their fear of looking like a cosmetics salesgirl in a department store leads them to shy away from make-up totally. As anyone over the age of 30 should know, not wearing concealer isn't the gateway to fresh-faced beauty – it's the signpost to wrinkles, broken veins and bags. Not that the bumpkin beauties should be downhearted. We promise that it's possible to wear a ton of make-up and look like your skin is fresh, flawless and free of any help. Cheeks can have a natural out-door glow made by Estée Lauder and eyelashes can look as long and lush as those of a dairy cow without piling on the mascara.

Like clothes, make-up is subject to changing trends. Unless you plan on taking to the catwalk, we suggest you leave extreme looks well alone and find a core make-up routine that can be added to for glamour and subtracted from for rambling.

A face shouldn't be seen as a blank canvas upon which to paint but more a picture that needs restoration.

BEAUTY BLUNDERS

MOTORWAY BLUSHER

WRONG – TRINNY

• Using the brush that the blusher comes with; they're usually too small and blunt-ended
• Not blending cream blusher with fingers or a small sponge
• Using a colour given away in a promotion. Just because it was free doesn't mean it suits you
• Using your cheek bone as a ruler leaves a harsh unblended line

RIGHT – SUSANNAH

• Choose a colour that compliments your skin tone
• Invest in a good, soft, rounded brush
• Tap off excess from your brush before application
• Brush on blusher from cheek to hairline
• Cream blushers are best for hairy faces
• Smile when you apply to make sure you get a good coverage on the apple of your cheek
• Gradually build up the colour
• Don't forget to check the side view
• Blend, blend, blend. No hard lines please

THE FOUNDATION TIDE MARK

WRONG – SUSANNAH

• Choosing the colour from the bottle alone
• Using foundation to look healthy. Leave that to the blusher or fake tan
• Not using a mirror
• Not blending over the jaw line
• Rubbing foundation on to the face like moisturizer or sun cream, using both hands at the same time

RIGHT – TRINNY

• Always test foundation on your jaw line. Testing on your hand or wrist won't tell you anything
• Always make sure it is the closest shade to your skin
• Always blend over the neck and jaw
• Apply using only fingertips or a sponge
• Look in the mirror in natural and electric light and check it works in both

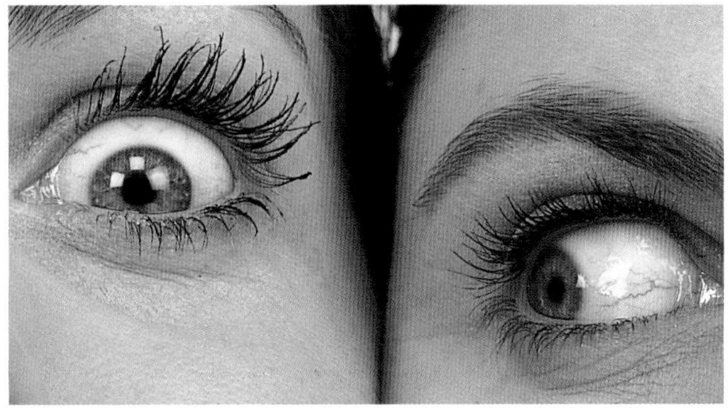

DRAG QUEEN LIP LINER

WRONG – SUSANNAH

- Choosing a lip liner that has no relationship with your lipstick
- Using too pointed or blunt a pencil
- Applying too much, too heavily
- Forgetting to blend in – never, ever show a lip line

RIGHT – TRINNY

- Choose a lip pencil the same colour as your lips for a natural look
- Choose a lip pencil the same colour as your lipstick for glamour
- Apply from the outer edges and work inwards
- Apply over a wax base if you have a feathering problem

GLOBBY MASCARA

WRONG – TRINNY

This look is often seen on the girl who 'can't live without her mascara' – it would be the one essential item on her desert island. Her eyelashes are so stiff that they could be plucked out and used to pin a poster to the wall.

- Buying cheap mascara – especially if it's labelled smudge free and waterproof
- Putting on mascara straight from the tube
- Applying too thickly

RIGHT – SUSANNAH

- Take out the brush and wipe with tissue before applying
- Apply slowly. It's the quick fix that will give lumps
- For a really professional approach apply in sections with the tip of the brush
- For a better shape, use an eyelash curler NOT more mascara
- For a very natural look, curl and separate with a clear brow gel
- Apply less or none on lower lashes, unless Malcolm McDowell in *A Clockwork Orange* is a look you admire
- For almond eyes, add a little extra at the edges
- Chuck mascara as soon as it begins to stink like a dirty flannel. It means it's gone off and dried out

BEAUTY BLUNDERS

EYEBROWS

WRONG – SUSANNAH

- Making the shape longer than your natural eyebrow
- Using too sharp a pencil
- Using a colour darker than your eyebrow shade
- Dying your eyebrows too dark
- Plucking them too thin

RIGHT – TRINNY

- Never take the line further than the outer edge of your eye socket
- Fill in brow, as opposed to drawing it on
- Use a blunt hard brush and eye shadow or brow powder to shape – not a pencil
- Use a colour close to the darkest shade of your natural hair colour
- Don't over-pluck

EYE SHADOW

WRONG – TRINNY

- Choosing a blue the colour of the sky – and thinking that it makes your blue eyes bluer
- Not blending
- Using the same colour all over the eye lid
- Wearing the same eye make-up for 20 years

RIGHT – SUSANNAH

- The colour of blue eyes is brought out by heather or brown, not bright blue
- Powdered shadow is more natural than cream and lasts longer
- Blending is the only way when applying shadow
- Use eye shadow to shape, not colour

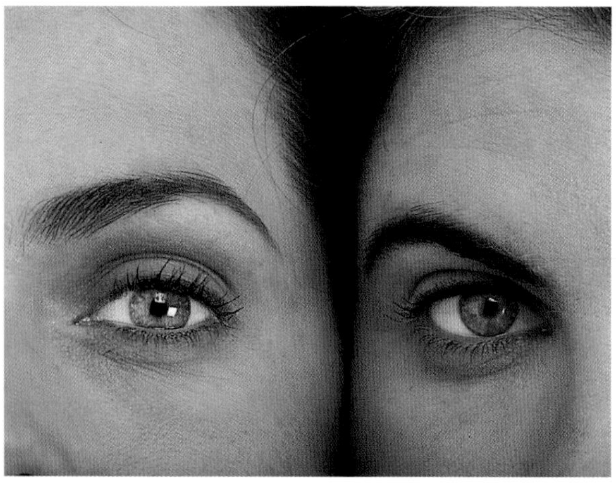

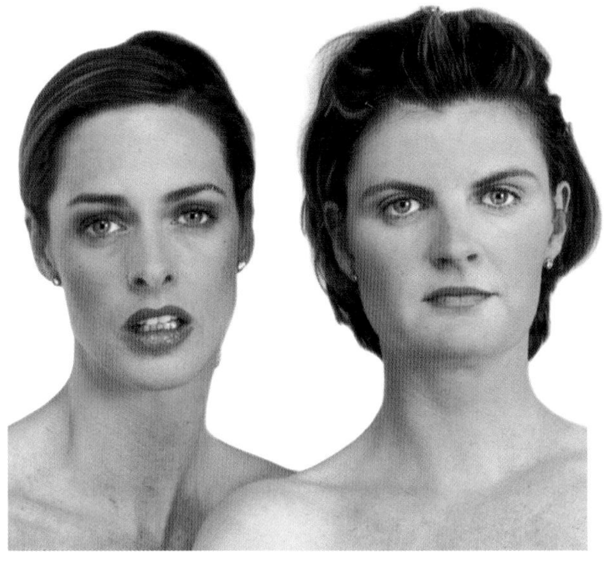

EYELINER

WRONG – TRINNY

• Ringing eyes with black lines à la Bette Davis in the film *Whatever Happened to Baby Jane?* or Diana in the *Panorama* TV interview
• Not blending
• Using liquid liner underneath as well as on top
• Wearing eyeliner inside eye with nothing else
• Wearing blue eyeliner

RIGHT – SUSANNAH

• For powder, use a fine brush and blend right in to the roots of upper eyelashes
• If using a pencil, blend thoroughly
• Keep liner on upper lid as close to lashes as possible
• Use only a minimal amount of eyeliner – to complement smoky shadow under lower lashes

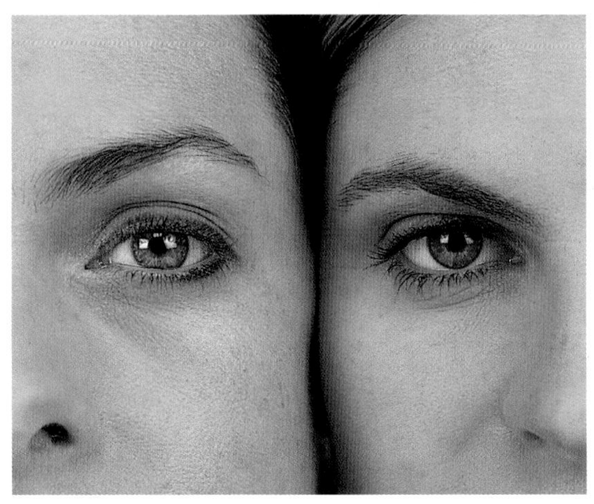

BRONZING

WRONG – SUSANNAH

• That orange hue
• Too much
• No respect for facial contours
• Putting it on under foundation
• Forgetting you have a neck that needs tanning too
• Forgetting it gathers around the eyebrow and moustache area

RIGHT – TRINNY

• Tap off the excess before applying liberally
• Put more on the prominent features that would get extra attention from the sun
• Blend into the hairline
• Remember the ears
• Wipe off the moustache and eyebrows
• Check it looks OK in natural daylight
• Don't go to sleep in it – for the sake of both your pores and the sheets

SKIN

HOW TO ACHIEVE A FLAWLESS FINISH

CONCEALER

- Start with a clean face. Look at it in a good, clear light and observe what needs concealing: dark circles, broken veins
- Pay special attention to shadows under eyes, blemishes around nose and mouth
- If you have obvious bags, use a concealer in a lighter shade than your foundation. Place on the bag and blend below the bag, not up to the eye, otherwise you will emphasize the puffiness
- If you suffer from dark circles, use a concealer in a lighter shade but sweep it up towards the eye
- Combat redness with a smooth, lavish sweep of concealer. Dab with fingers for the most natural finish

COVERING SPOTS

- Use a concealer brush to apply cover-up
- Use the same shade as your foundation
- Make sure the product doesn't dry out over your spot (check the texture when buying). This will cause flaking and show up the pimple even more
- Don't squeeze spots before making up. You might think this will eradicate the zit but in fact it will result in the pus and weeping ruining your concealing efforts

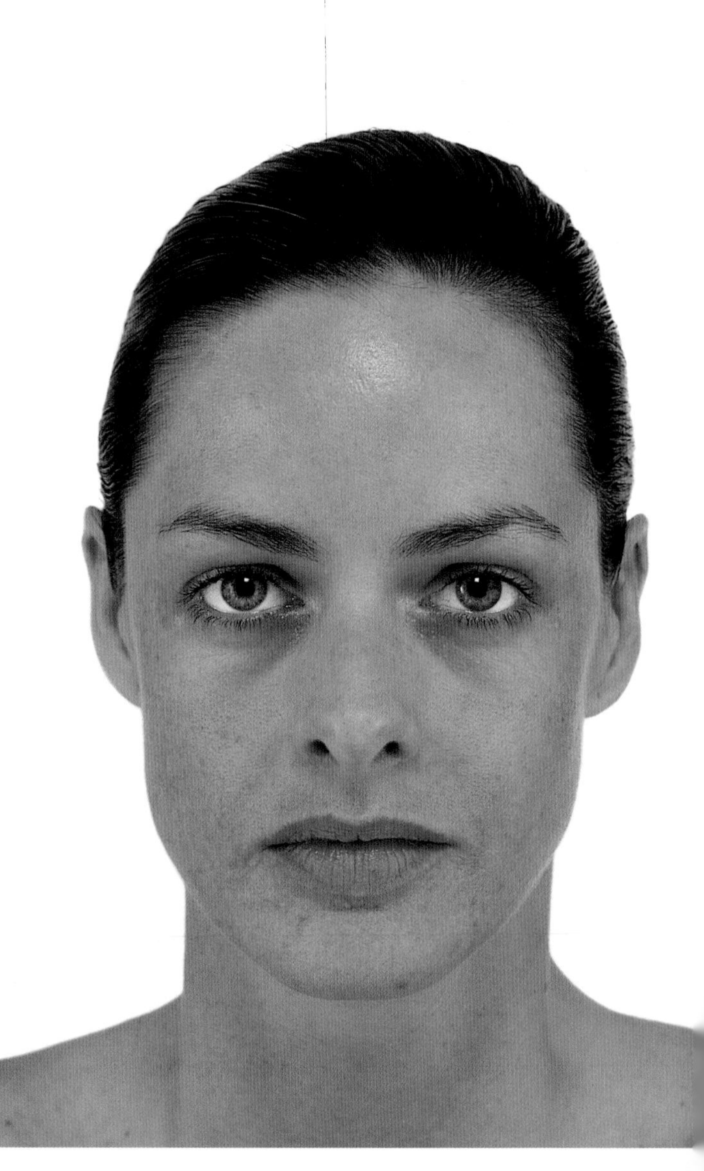

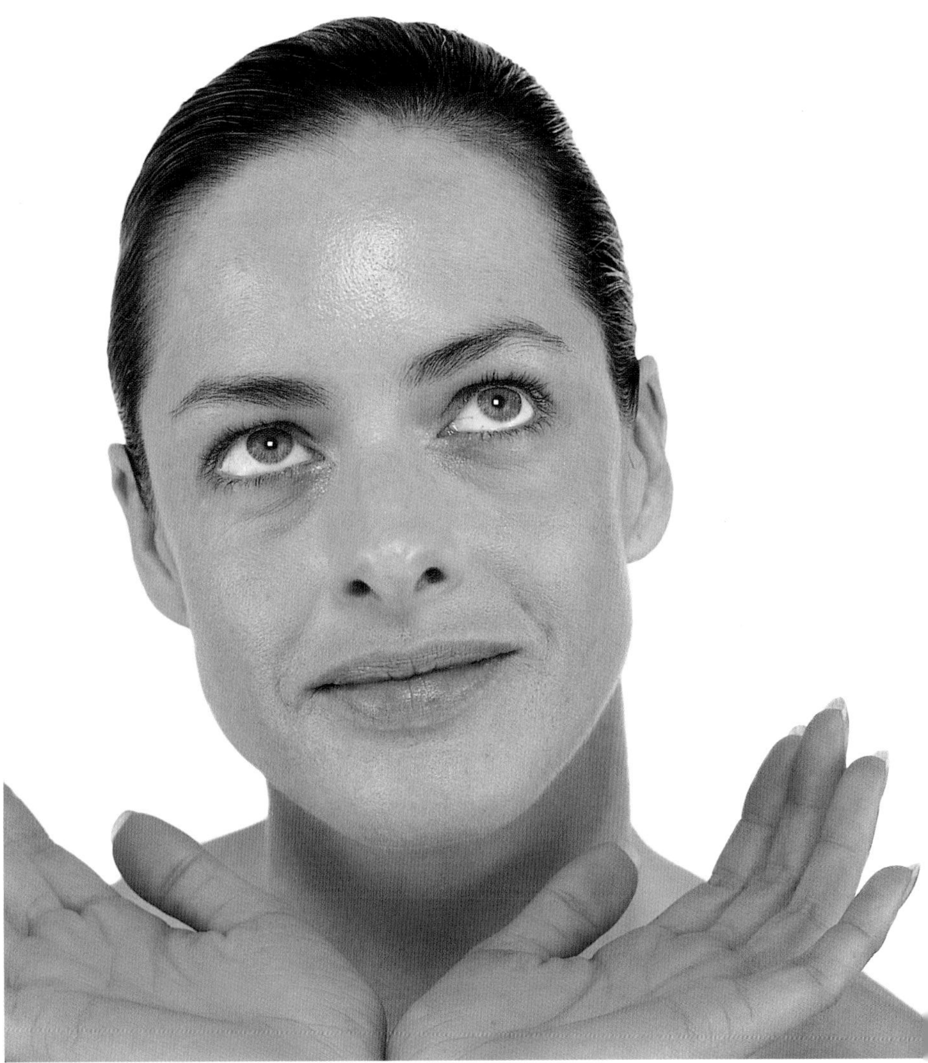

FOUNDATION

- Choose a shade that exactly matches your skin tone
- If you have used the right amount of concealer you won't need so much foundation
- Usually you will need more foundation where you have uneven skin tone or redness, particularly in the T-zone (forehead, nose and chin)
- For a light finish, blend very well, using a sponge or your fingertips
- Good loose powder is essential to keep foundation in place all day. Try to find a powder without too much talc, otherwise your skin will dry out
- Apply with a nice big powder puff. Shake off excess before rolling the powder-laden puff on your face. Brush face downwards with a big powder brush
- Don't keep your powder puff with your powder, otherwise it will become caked with loose powder and you will always end up using too much

Brand	Product	Who for
BeneFit	Boi-ing! (concealer)	Everyone
BeneFit	Lemon-aid (eyelid colour corrector)	Everyone
Bobbi Brown	Foundation stick	Oily skins
Laura Mercier	Moisturizing foundation	Dry skins
Shu Uemura	Loose powder	Everyone

CHEEKS

HOW TO GAIN A GLOWING COMPLEXION

- Remember, blusher should make you look healthy, not painted
- First, prepare your skin. Even out blotches with a concealer that matches your skin tone
- Pay special attention to things that make you look tired, for example circles under the eyes, tram lines around the mouth. For these, use a concealer that is a shade lighter than your skin tone
- Buy blusher to suit your skin type:

  dry skin needs a cream blusher to give it a glowing, natural, healthy look

  oily skin doesn't need extra shine, so choose a powder blusher
- Decide on your blush colour: for blooming cheeks it's best to use a browny-pink tone. The effect you want is that of having come in from a brisk walk in the country as opposed to an exuberant dance in a nightclub
- A dab of blusher on the end of your nose makes for an extra healthy glow
- Don't over-powder shiny skin. A little glow gives a healthy impression

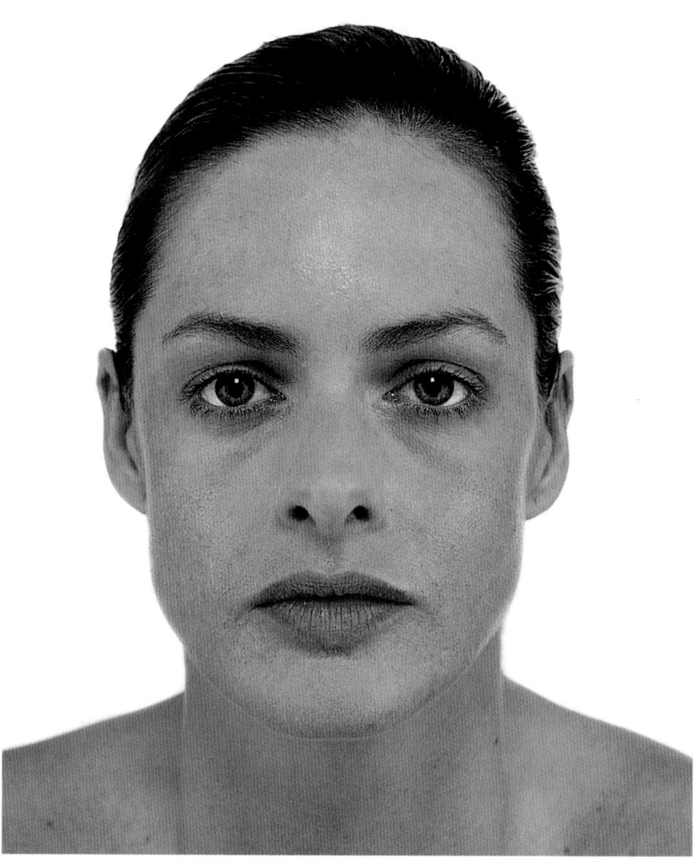

Brand	**Product**	**Who for**
Origins	Pinch Your Cheeks gel	Every skin type
Bobbi Brown	Cream blush stick	Dry skins
BeneFit	Benetint	Those who know how to apply
Yves St Laurent	Touche Eclat (highlighter)	Everyone

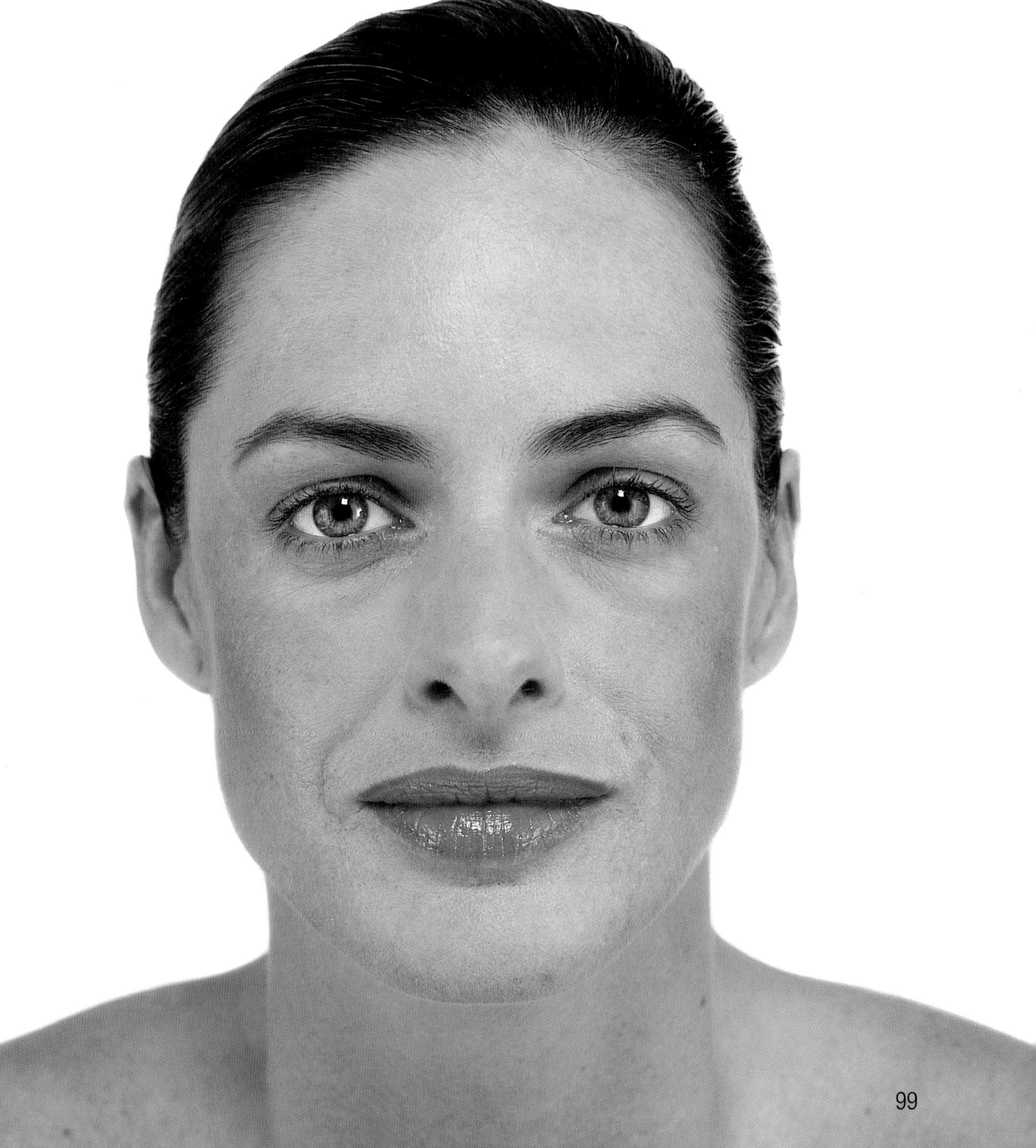

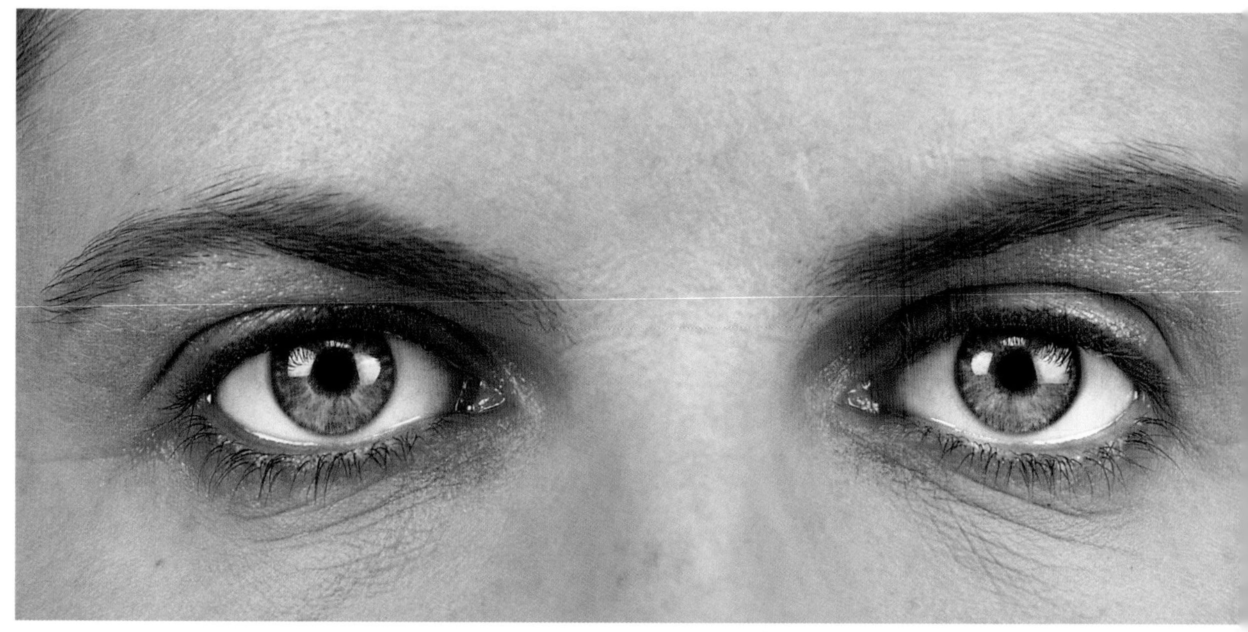

BROWS

HOW TO BRIGHTEN YOUR EYES

- A well plucked eyebrow changes your whole eye for the better
- Pluck well above the eye to create space between the brow and lid
- Whatever the natural shape of your eye, follow it
- NEVER over-pluck. A thicker but shaped brow is the most natural
- When filling in sparse areas of brow, use a powder and not a pencil. It's less harsh and easier to apply
- Some brows need to be slightly extended at the outer corner. This broadens the face and balances out the whole eye area

Brand	Product	What it does
Tweezerman	Tweezers	Opens up the upper lid; a well-shaped brow makes all the difference
BeneFit	Eyebright pencil	Opens up the eye without looking chalky
BeneFit	Lemon-aid (highlighter and colour corrector)	Opens up upper lid and allows eye make-up to glide on

EYES

- Find an eye shadow in a tone that is close to your skin colour. It's not about colouring in the eye, more about contouring
- When applying eye make-up, look face on into a large mirror so that you can see your whole face
- Keep your eyes open when applying shadow. Put colour in an arch on the base of the brow bone. Don't put it too high
- Remember that darker colours make the eyes recede and paler ones push them forward. Use highlighter on brow bones to open up the eyes
- Before applying mascara, use an eyelash curler to open up the lashes
- To avoid clogging, wipe the mascara wand with tissue. It's better to apply two thin layers than one thick globby one

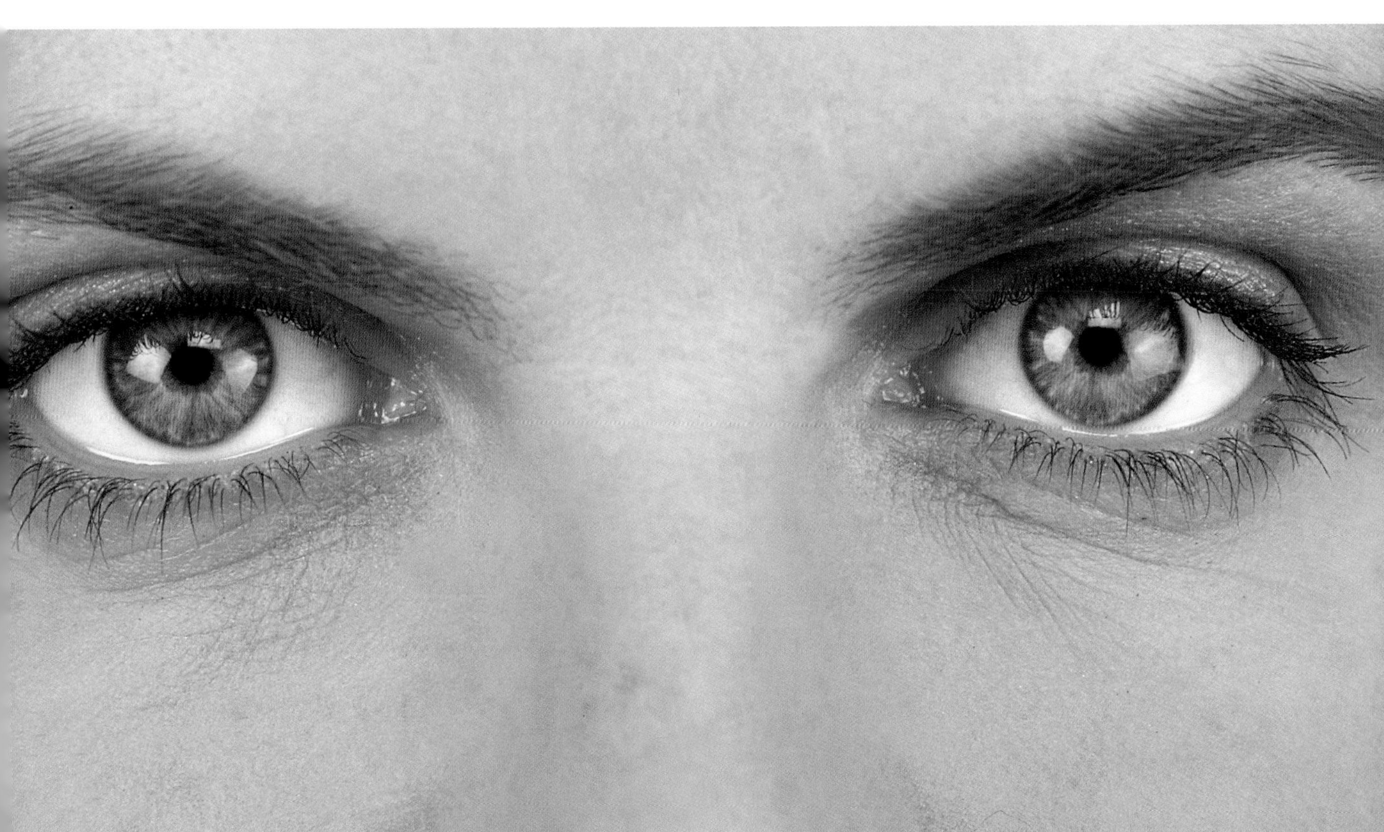

LIPS

HOW TO APPLY THE PERFECT POUT

1. Take a toothbrush and brush lips to get rid of dry skin
2. Cover with a tiny amount of Vaseline to prevent drying
3. Take a product that fills in the lip grooves (Guerlain's Lip Lift) and pass over the entire lip area
4. Take a staining product (Origin's Pinch Your Cheeks) and smooth onto lips from rim to rim. If you don't suffer from upper lip hair or your small lips could look bigger, extend the stain beyond the edge of the lip with a lip brush. Don't go overboard or you'll look like a kid who's been sucking on a sticky lollipop
5. Take a natural coloured lip pencil and outline your mouth. Use a lip brush to blend into the centre. Make sure the lip pencil is not one that leaves caking
6. Take a lip gloss in a shiny pale colour and apply to the centre of the lips to make them look bigger
7. If you want to make your lips appear smaller (who in their right mind does?) then apply a darker colour in the middle and a lighter colour on the outside
8. Finish off with a tiny dab of Vaseline for a full pout

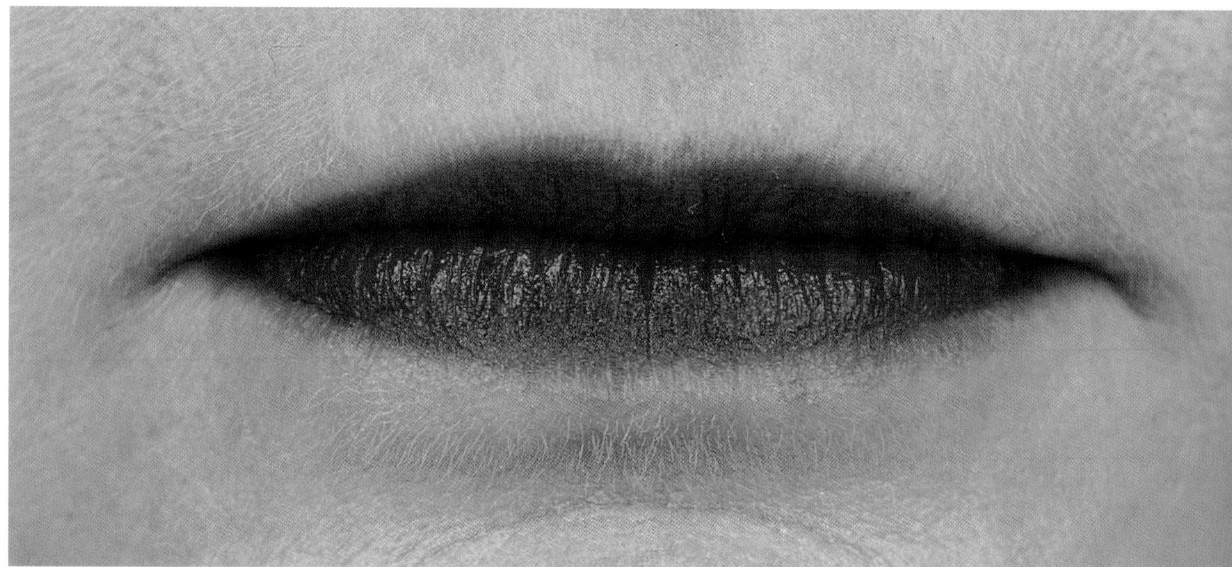

Brand	Product	What it does
Clinique	All About Lips	Helps with feathering problems
Guerlain	Lip Lift	Puffs out lips
Origins	Pinch Your Cheeks	Gives a natural lip colour: use a very small amount and apply with your fingertip. Go to the full outline of your lips or, if you don't suffer from lip hair, even outside the rim – keeping a very smooth line
Bobbi Brown	Natural lip pencil	Go around the edge of the colour, creating a good contrast between your skin and lips – blend into the centre of the mouth to avoid any lip line
Bobbi Brown	Shimmer lip gloss	Put a small amount in the centre of the lips to create a pouty mouth

WORKING

EVERYDAY MAKE-UP

• A primer (foundation base) is essential – this will help your make-up glide on and stay in place all day
• Use a foundation that gives good coverage and is not too oily, as this will slide off more quickly
• Remember that the lights you have to work under might be very different from those you use at home. Strip office lighting whites out most faces
• A bronzer will help you look healthier throughout the day and it can be re-applied without looking cakey. But remember that too much looks appalling and artificial. Try to find one that is more taupe than orange
• The alternative to a bronzed look is rosy cheeks. Careful with the application, as if it's not done from the apple of your cheeks to the hairline, it could look very unnatural. Try to remember how you look after a brisk, healthy walk in the country and apply in the same areas. It will look more natural
• Use eye colours that are natural but flattering. Powders are preferable, to avoid creasing in the eye socket, and are best applied over the base that you use for your foundation. Alternatively, apply a little face powder before application, so eye shadow lasts longer
• Shape your brows – use a powder rather than a pencil to avoid any harsh lines
• Many women feel that if they slap on a bit of bright lipstick they are all set to go and conquer the world – wrong. The colour is all-important: it should harmonize with the type of blusher/bronzer and eye make-up you are using

Left to right: Philosophy's The Present primer/oil-free moisturizer; Estée Lauder Double Wear foundation; La Prairie face powder; Stila lip pencil; Body Shop Colourings lipline fixer; Cosmetics A La Carte eye shadow palette; Maybelline Great Lash mascara; BeneFit Ooh La Lift – a firming and de-puffing highlighter that can be used over make-up

WEEKEND

THE NATURAL LOOK

- If cold weather makes your skin prone to redness, try a red-diffusing, green-tinted moisturizer (René Guinot anti-redness cream, Gatineau SOS Matisse green cream, Serge Louis Alvarez pre-make-up base)
- If you cover your entire face in foundation you will look over-made-up, something you want to avoid with your country cousins
- Instead of foundation, apply concealer only where you have spots, bags or red marks. Use the same colour as your skin tone, and choose a product that does not cake (and is not affected by wind and cold); try to test before you buy – a lot depends on whether your skin is oily, normal or dry
- Apply a natural-looking blusher in the places where you normally blush. Use a cream (Estée Lauder rose, Bobbi Brown soft plum) and apply a powder blusher over the top to prevent the cream from rubbing off
- Use a lip stain in a very natural or minimal colour. Sometimes Vaseline can bring out your natural colour and look great
- Don't use mascara as it will inevitably run in damp air and you will end up resembling a panda. Instead, use a clear eyebrow gel to subtly lengthen your eyelashes. Or consider getting them dyed
- Remember, if you look pale during the day and your make-up bag isn't handy, pinch your cheeks hard for a country maiden 'I've just been laid' look

Left to right: Serge Louis Alvarez pre-make-up base; Lancôme concealer and colour correcting palette; Chantecaille translucent foundation; Dr Hauschka lip and cheek stain; Body Shop Colourings clear brow and lash gel; Bobbi Brown Essentials cream blush; Clinique Clear Lip moisture stick

NIGHTTIME

EVENING MAKE-UP

• Try to anticipate the lighting and prepare your face accordingly. For example, if it is a summer event and you will still be in daylight, do your make-up by the window in natural light
• This doesn't mean, however, that if you are going to a sexy, dark nightclub, you should do your make-up in a dark room; there is still the journey there and back – wherever that might end up
• Begin with foundation primer, to help keep foundation on all night
• If you decide to focus on full, glossy lips, keep eye make-up simple so you don't look overdone
• Use a lipstick fixing product to keep lip colour in place while drinking and kissing
• Don't take your entire make-up bag for touch-ups: you should be carrying only a small evening purse. Cut down your pencils and take sample sizes of products – often given away as promotional offers from cosmetic houses. Many companies like Shu Uemura and Muji sell small containers into which you can transfer your foundation and powders

Left to right: Laura Mercier foundation primer; Chantecaille cream foundation – will not cake, even after sweaty dancing; Bobbi Brown Essentials concealer; Yves St Laurent Touche Eclat highlighter for eyes – apply as a touch-up between dinner and dancing; Francoise Nars highlighter – apply to cheeks to catch the light when clubbing; Ruby & Millie eyebrow shadow and wax – well-defined eyebrows frame and set off face; Chanel eye shadow compact in subtle silvery greys; Lancôme mascara; Clinique All About Lips – will keep lipstick on and prevent feathering; Guerlain Lip Lift – to plump up lips for a sexy, seductive pout; Chantecaille lipstick; Bobbi Brown shimmer lip gloss

GLAMOUR

MAKE-UP FOR SPECIAL OCCASIONS

Both of us have taken a long time to get used to wearing a glamorous face at special occasions. It takes a lot of confidence and practice to achieve this look without ending up appearing a trifle tarty

- Base your look on colours that you know suit you for daytime and nighttime and then enhance them
- Remember the cardinal rule of a glamorous face – focus on the lips or the eyes BUT NOT BOTH; this will lead to a very over-made-up face that does not focus on either feature
- If you are going for sexy, come-hither eyes, remember the importance of blending – there should be no harsh lines to your powder however strong the depth of colour. If you blend well, nothing will stand out unnaturally
- If you opt for strong eyes, the lips should look full but very natural, with only a hint of colour. However, this should not prevent you doing your best to make them look as full as possible (see the section on lips, page 102)
- If you are going for full colour, pouty lips, play down the eyes.

We are talking about the 'no make-up' make-up look. It will take as long to apply but the effects will be very natural and will bring out the colour and shape of your eyes.

Left to right: Matis skin enhancing base to set make-up in place; Laura Mercier foundation – not too heavy-looking; Laura Mercier Secret Concealer palette; Lancôme eye shadow compact; Hard Candy eyeliner; Bobbi Brown Essentials lip pencil in nude, for natural-looking lips; Stila mascara; Bobbi Brown Essentials lipstick; Estée Lauder powder compact – dinky size, pretty enough to take out at dinner

SUMMARY

If your body feels great, you'll wear your prescribed wardrobe with more confidence. No spots will mean less make-up, a new haircut will require less maintenance. Once you have deciphered the problems, prioritize them in order of hatefulness and tackle them one by one. When one physical obstacle has been resolved you'll find yourself encouraged to take on the rest.

Once you have mastered the most important element, a great-looking skin, this will act as a canvas upon which to experiment with different looks.

We have recommended certain products that we feel really stand out above their competitors. There are cheaper products, but we feel it's more sensible to save up for cosmetics that do what they promise.

Over the years we have changed our make-up as we have learnt more about application and the qualities of certain products. Our increased confidence has enabled us to wear more at night and we have had huge fun experimenting on each other. It takes balls to wear bold dramatic make-up, so first time round do it with a friend.

THE TEN COMMANDMENTS

1. Remember, a beauty problem looks worse to us, because it's all we see in the mirror.
2. Most beauty dilemmas are solvable – as long as you are prepared to be disciplined.
3. It's not bollocks when hairdressers say a new haircut can change your life.
4. Good deportment goes a long way to instantly losing five pounds – don't let your fat flip over the top of your bikini.
5. 'Flawless' skin is everything.
6. Less is more with make-up. Piling on the make-up to look healthier makes you look like an ill person underneath.
7. If you have worn the same make-up for five years, it's time for a change.
8. Too much make-up at work prevents people seeing past your face.
9. For perfect nighttime looks, remember to focus on the eyes or lips but NEVER both.
10. It's less important how much you spend on a product, more about how you apply it. Many of the best solutions are free.

5

CULLING

Phew, I'm
shagged out

INTRODUCTION

We are all guilty of having orphan garments in our wardrobes. Unworn clothes are a waste of space and need to be culled. There is no earthly reason for keeping a jersey, however old a friend, if you never wear it.

Much of what we clutter the shelves with is kept either because it cost the earth or for sentimental reasons; these are the most difficult pieces to let go of. Some things might just be there out of habit – you've got used to them. These too need re-evaluation.

It helps enormously to have a friend over when you cut the ties. She can give a ruthless and objective opinion. If you can't see that a white lace dress makes you look vast, she can.

Though an emotional experience, the upside of savage culling is immense. It paves the way for new clothes, brings in cash from cast-out pieces that you can sell, and those that you can't will give warmth to people in need. The therapeutic value peaks upon finding a dress you forgot all about.

We know it's not easy to chuck clothes, but take heart from the knowledge that there is no downside to a selective cull.

BRAS

Bust dimensions change more than any other part of the body: weight fluctuation, time of the month and pregnancy wreak havoc with a cup size. Fit is of paramount importance and there is no earthly reason to give drawer space to a bra that doesn't flatter. What you do need are bras for specific roles. A sports boulder holder is not appropriate for a ball gown and a lacy push up is all too evidently wrong for a T-shirt.

- The sexy bra – the one where the lace is so cumbersome that it can't be worn underneath anything without your tits looking like a mole field
- The sports bra – this is the one that's been washed to buggery. It's gone grey, always looks dirty and must cause you embarrassment in the changing room
- The T-shirt bra – gives great smooth lines but its lack of support leaves your tits down by your navel
- The everyday bra – just because it's for everyday does not mean it shouldn't flatter. Lift them up and push them out girl, you never know who might be in the bus queue or loitering in the fresh fruit aisle
- The padded bra – your tits are too small and you were very over-optimistic when you bought it. Whenever you put it on for a sexy seductive evening, you need to fill it with tissue paper

WHY KEPT?	**WHY CHUCK?**
First bra	But you are a double D now
Lactating bra	It's stained with milk
Valentine's present	It's bright red
Gives a great shape from the front	Digs into skin at back
It's part of a set	But you still haven't found the knickers
It gives my boobs the best uplift	The under-wiring has popped out

KNICKERS

If there is one drawer that resists being opened because it is so full, it's the knicker drawer. For some reason, however many pairs we have, we are always buying more. Sooner or later these too will get stained by various secretions and will join the ranks in the knicker graveyard. Horrid knickers imply an unclean personality, so no matter what the cost, ALWAYS have fresh underpants. When buying matching underwear, you will need three or four pairs of knickers to go with a bra.

- The granny knickers – many moons ago, these will have started out brilliantly comfortable and covering everything. They have since become a mini brief which is not your school of panty
- The mini brief – these are in no man's land. No man will ever go near them and they neither fully cover nor are brief enough for a smooth finish
- The bikini briefs – almost entirely responsible for the VPL
- The cheese wire, a.k.a. the G-string. Despite its saucy connotations, this is a highly practical garment: the right size should give good cover up front and VPL-freedom from behind. If you have cellulite on your ass, please stick to the granny knicker when wearing fine fabrics
- The French or cami knickers – useless at catching discharge and ride right up your crack. Bedroom clothing, not underclothing

WHY KEPT?	**WHY CHUCK?**
Laziness	Any knicker that looks worn, stained, too small or too saggy must be chucked
Comfort	The period stain did not quite come out
Sentimental value: they've got hearts, bunnies or Pooh bear on them	The elastic's gone

T-SHIRTS

The most prolifically collected item in a woman's wardrobe. Over the years there will be a build-up of souvenir specials, vest imposters, childhood memories and oversized ones used for bed or the beach. Most will need ejecting. As we have shown in a previous chapter, because a T-shirt is an item we survive by, it needs to be the perfect shape for you. Don't digress or be tempted by a picture of the Eiffel Tower unless it's going to flatter.

- The big baggy – so many women resort to this as a cover-up for bodily defects. The baggy T-shirt is, however, a far greater act of immorality than anything it is hiding. The one good thing is that it will make a fabulous duster
- The childhood friend – this can be kept if it is in a pretty colour and nicely faded, but white ones will not have lasted the course of time and should be chucked. Stretched or shrunken items will look precisely what they are – old
- The holiday souvenir – if bought as a cool T-shirt in its own right that's fine, but if it suffers from the name of a hotel, city or country in garish colours, chuck it out
- The tight white – this T-shirt can be too tight. If you can see the lumps on your areola you know it's time for a change

WHY KEPT?	**WHY CHUCK?**
It's nice around the body	Ragged around the neck
The perfect T-shirt	Aside from the deodorant stains that are now burning through with the ferocity of acid
It's new	But navy never suited you
For DIY days	Didn't we see the builders in your house last week?

JUMPERS

This is probably the second largest collection in your wardrobe and definitely not all your own. Brother's, ex-boyfriend's, dad's...for some miraculous reason each seemed the perfect jumper when you nicked it. Just remember that ill-fitting cardigans and jumpers are the easiest way to add lumps to your outline and bump up your size.

- Cashmere – with a reputation for luxury, cashmere is hard to let go of. It's expensive, but we get good use from it by wearing it non-stop. Sadly, its popularity shows. It's balled and bagged and too much dry-cleaning has made it hard – time for retirement
- Cotton – thick cotton knits are too bulky for summer yet not warm enough for winter; they are downright unflattering and should never have been purchased. Fine cotton cardigans are the only way to go
- Wool – people think the larger the jersey the warmer it's going to be. Wrong. In future, buy one cashmere to your ten woollens, keeping a couple of old sods for rain-soaked walks and manual work in the winter
- The loud, big-patterned jersey – by attacking this we know we might offend lovers of pretty pretty knitwear the world over, but we feel strongly that a jersey should never make too loud a statement. The shouting should be left to other items

WHY KEPT?	**WHY CHUCK?**
Knitted by my granny	She died three years ago
Cashmere	Hole under arm from industrial-strength deodorant
Old friend	Peppered with moth holes
The only one to go with designer skirt	It shrunk, and no strength in the world will stretch it back to its original shape
Just in case	What about the other 20?

TOPS

Although we have put the spotlight on T-shirts and sweaters, there is a whole continent of other garments suitable for our top halves. A spangly boob tube may be considered a collector's item, but the majority of sentimental keepsakes must go.

- The classic white shirt – unless it is pristine it can very quickly become like those regulation school shirts that have been washed one too many times
- Shirts – attractive as a weekend filler. Personally we think they are wholly unfeminine and should be left to men
- Silk T-shirts – these snag like tights, stretch and bag like wet wool and only look nice on the flat-chested or more mature lady
- Waistcoats – ooh, here's a dodgy one. These must only come out if fashion permits, otherwise be sure no one is aware of their presence in your wardrobe
- Tunics – these do hide a multitude of sins, but are completely hopeless for anyone with big tits
- Halternecks – if skin and muscles sag, wrinkle or are anything other than granite hard, you must ban these from your body

WHY KEPT?	WHY CHUCK?
White T-shirt, looks fab with jeans	That ink stain will never come out
Silk T-shirt, great under jackets	Deodorant has burnt into fabric
Halterneck is a great shape for me	You can't wear a bra with it, and it's time you did, so chuck it
I love this shirt, and it still smells of him	He left you, leave his shirt in the bin

TROUSERS

These find their way into every section of a wardrobe, some folded, some hanging, many not worn, and your favourites always seem to get hidden. People tend to always buy the same shape and colour, but how many black pairs do you really need?

- The tailored trouser – pleated at the top and narrowing down to a tapered leg does nothing at all for the pear-shaped woman. Our most hated piece of clothing
- Jeans – in spite of perhaps having bought more than one pair in your quest for the perfect jeans, you always go back to your favourites. What are the others taking up space in your wardrobe for?
- Horror jeans – stone-washed, skintight drainpipe, rip-off designer jeans, true designer jeans with studs and/or rhinestones. In our experience these have never flattered anybody
- Slacks – the word says it all. The cornerstone of every lazy woman's wardrobe before leggings were invented. Only OK if dark, bootleg and used as substitute casual trousers

WHY KEPT?	**WHY CHUCK?**
They go with everything	Except your body shape
Good for every day	They have pleats at the front
Designer label	Need to lie down to do up the zip
The fabric is unique	Rides up your crack
Hip hipsters	You know your hips are too wide

SKIRTS

Light and frothy summer skirts are too easy to buy. You can find divine little slips on the high street, which means they can be bought in bulk more than most headline garments. Fit isn't essential unless it's pencil shape or bias-cut, where the cheaper skirts tend to have low-grade side seams that buckle, but resist a gathered waist at any price, no matter how alluring the fabric.

- The suit skirt – you have only ever worn it as part of a suit. You discarded the jacket a long time ago, thinking the skirt would work on its own, but it's too structured and boring to be a stand alone piece
- The short skirt – if you're over 30, anything above mid thigh is sad and cheap, not sexy and enticing. Even opaque tights won't save it
- The short skirt 2 – if your thighs have a gap in between when you push your knees together, you have the legs for a short skirt
- The bias-cut skirt – if you have put on weight and the skirt still seems to fit, check that it's still long enough: the more fabric required to cover a bigger ass, the less left in the length
- The stained skirt – that indelible grease spot: you know it's there, even if no one else does. The consequence is you never wear it
- The broken-zip skirt – if you really loved this skirt, you would have got the zip fixed years ago. It will never happen
- The floral floater with elastic waist – our disdain for this undeservedly popular skirt will offend many women. Ladies, buck up, it makes you look provincial and dull

WHY KEPT?	**WHY CHUCK?**
It made you feel slim	But can you get into it now?
Expensive velvet skirt.	It was never meant to be crushed velvet
Lovely white skirt.	The slip needed will make it frumpy
It's light and gorgeous	We can see your cellulite through it

JACKETS

Apart from sports and weatherproof jackets we feel that short coats are generally a more versatile and modern solution. For a jacket to look good it needs to be skilfully cut and this means expensive. It's fine if the jacket is part of a favoured suit, but stand-alone jackets are often ill fitting and have a hard time finding mates.

- The blazer – the backbone of many women's wardrobes. A classic when worn with jeans or tailored trousers, a disaster when worn with a full, flowing skirt. As it's probably worn incessantly, make sure it does not have that over-dry-cleaned sheen
- The velvet jacket – if it's marked, it's out. No dry-cleaner can ever make velvet look new again
- The linen jacket – whatever the quality, you always end up looking like a man in one of these. Linen mix sometimes prevents creasing
- The bomber – the best way to hide a waist and make your legs look shorter. This will never be a flattering style. We cannot recommend it remaining in anyone's wardrobe. We wore them in the early eighties and cringe at the memory
- The jean jacket – same principal as jeans. The older the better, though dark blue denim does come in and out of fashion. Stone wash is not even a contender. Blouson style with buckles on the side of the hem is criminal
- The leather – biker babes aren't meant to have style, just protection, so they can hang on to their biker jackets. Flying jackets on women are ghastly, as are any blouson style leathers. Anything other than fitted or skintight leather should be hung by neck not hanger
- Waterproof/sports jacket – worth keeping, to lend to friends

WHY KEPT?	**WHY CHUCK?**
Galliano classic.	From 15 years ago
It's a great shape	Because of the shoulder pads?
My waist looks tiny	Double-breasted makes your tits look vast
Bargain.	But it's patterned

DRESSES

Dresses are a one-item outfit that makes them incredibly useful. However, finding the right shape for you can take time, and may lead to mistakes bought out of frustration. The wrong style wreaks havoc on the body. It is easier to look horrendous in a dress than anything else, so take heed of the following advice.

- The sleeveless shift dress – you need to be cigarette slim for this. If your shift is in a size 12 or over, you cannot wear it. Susannah can't be seen dead in one
- The 'fat day' dress. There's nothing wrong with a floaty A-line unless it's in an unflattering colour. On days when you need to hide your body, do you want to compound the problem by looking sallow and tired because you are wearing a skin-killing shade? These are far nicer in soft colours
- The short evening dress – one of these is essential, but it mustn't be too short, mustn't be too glitzy and – God forbid – it mustn't be patterned
- The sundress – these are not governed by fashion. You might have some you've owned for donkey's years. It's okay to keep all but the grubbiest, as long as the older ones are reserved for beach holidays

WHY KEPT?	WHY CHUCK?
It's your favourite wedding outfit.	Everyone's seen it
You remember the pain of the cost.	It will never come back in fashion
By a hot new designer	It never suited you in the first place
Your favourite colour	Your worst shape
It belonged to your mum.	Why did she give it to you?

COATS

Why do we assume that a coat will come back into fashion and therefore hang onto it just in case? It's a commonly held opinion that coats should last forever, which is why we see some women wearing coats that could do with a good brush up. Another popular misconception is that because a coat covers all, we can wear any shape we want. Coats are like the window to your personal style, so for God's sake keep only the very best.

- The old timer – like your best friend, everyone needs one, but keep it for dog walking and country pursuits. There is no need to have more than one (tell that to Susannah)
- The classic – simple and elegant. If you have found the one for you, look after it well, as these are hard to find
- The evening coat – another collectable item. The ones that are handed down from granny are usually the best, but watch out for frayed brocade, moth-eaten fur and blotchy velvet: all should be discarded
- The winter coat – you probably only buy one of these every five years, but as it's your mainstay garment for the winter months, shouldn't you spend proportionately more and change it more often?
- Macs – hands up who has a flattering mac? We do need these, but never wear a mac as a fashion item, only to keep the rain off

WHY KEPT?	WHY CHUCK?
There will never be one to replace it	It's so worn it has bald patches
It keeps me warm	It is possible to look smart and warm
It covers everything	A long coat should be very long. There is nothing worse than a three-quarter length
My friends love it	They suit wide lapels, you don't

SHOES

Many women collect shoes like children collect stamps. They clutter up hallways and cupboard floors and get shoved under beds and hidden behind furniture by dogs and children. The truth is that 90% haven't been worn for years, if ever. In preparing to rid yourself of all but the remaining 10%, lay out the shoes in the categories shown below and give each pair an honest and searching appraisal.

- Pavement shoes – there are going to be many old friends here that should have gone a long time ago. They'll be scuffed at the toe and wrinkled like a walnut. While a heel can always be resoled, a creased upper can never be restored
- House shoes – the older they are the more comfortable they become. They usually start life as pavement shoes. They are allowed to be slightly trashed because they'll not be going out in public. If they smell or are so worn you can't keep them on your foot, it's time to say goodbye. Sorrrry!
- Trainers – these begin life in the gym. They then start to disintegrate and become walking shoes. This is the time to buy a new pair for the gym… and so the rotation continues
- High-heeled day shoes – how many of you have a pair of shoes with a heel that needs fixing? It's either dropped off or the leather has started to peel back, revealing the white plastic underneath. If they've reached this stage of disrepair it's likely you'll never get them sorted. Out they go
- Evening shoes – these date speedily because they are subject to fashion changes more than any other shoe. If they are bland enough to go with everything, then they are too dull and should be chucked anyway. The rest are likely to have been bought at great expense and in an assortment of wild colours that bear no resemblance to anything hanging in your wardrobe. Or they are too high and you will never feel confident enough to wear them. Either way it's into the bin liner

WHY KEPT?	WHY CHUCK?
A work of art	Picturesque, yes, but half a size too small
Expensive	Very dated
A bargain	Wrong shape for leg
Fun fashionable colour	But you don't suit acid green

HANDBAGS

Bagladies of the world unite, you have nothing to lose but your chains. Some women have a bag for every outfit; inevitably they end up locking themselves out because they forgot to transfer their keys to the right bag. At the opposite end of the scale is the one-bag woman, whose gigantic sack weighs her down day and night.

- Big leather friend – it's scratched and scuffed and you can never find anything in it
- The fabric bag – stained with ink from a leaky Biro, or just very grubby
- The black leather clutch – with optional gold clasp. It's not big enough for the day and too heavy for the evening
- The frayed basket – with one handle that has gone or is about to go
- Freebie make-up bag (posing as evening bag) – black zip-up canvas or, at a push, satin clutch – you bought the products and you got the bag
- Evening bag – you've had since your first kiss at a party. Like Trinny's, it might be black quilted velvet with embroidery and gold tassels. YUK!
- Cheap briefcase – where the cardboard is showing through the leatherette. At your first job interview it didn't make a strong impression, so why is it still there?
- The quilted bag – still popular, in spite of being the archetypal yuppie relic of the money-grabbing eighties
- The gold chain strap bag – another relic of the eighties that should have been left there
- The navy blue leather bag – falls into the cotton jersey and blouson leather jacket brigade. The blandest bag of all
- Bum bag – horrid even in the danger zone of Bolivia

WHY KEPT?	WHY CHUCK?
It's still got things inside you might need	Put those things into a new bag
It's the perfect match for your 'weddings' outfit	Threw the dress out three pages ago
Usually kept in a high inaccessible cupboard	You obviously don't care about it, having not laid eyes on it for ten years
It took you ages to save up for it	By the time you had saved up the fad was over

EVENING GOWNS

Because the evening dress is usually an expensive garment, it remains in the cupboard for years. If you buy simple, it can be a classic that stands the test of our ruthlessness, but how many of you can't stand the sight of your froufrou frock and long for something new?

- The Laura Ashley cotton – are you still at school?
- Tartan taffeta – Sloanesville
- The antique – it might be beautifully beaded and have a designer label, it may have belonged to your great aunt, but if it doesn't suit you, you shouldn't wear it, so give it to your sister/cousin/niece
- Frills and flounces – if your gown resembles anything on the cover of a Barbara Cartland novel, save for a replacement now
- The perfect dress (with a red wine stain) – the stain reminds you of a fun evening, but spoils the dress – have the dress dyed a darker colour and give it a new lease of life

WHY KEPT?	**WHY CHUCK?**
Your daughter might like it	Not if she wants to be fashionable
It's so useful.	It's so dated
Black lace makes me feel elegant . .	It doubles your size
It's tight, it's sexy	You are too old for this
I will wear it again,one day.	This year? Next year? Sometime? Never!

JEWELLERY

Fake jewellery is cheap and therefore collectable. As little girls, our pocket money was spent on it once we had graduated from sweeties. During our own cull, we found pieces that had been around since the seventies. Each period in our lives seemed to have a different jewellery box containing an assortment of bedraggled and dated baubles. The exorcism was a highly satisfying process.

- Necklaces – any that need re-stringing should take the fast track to a charity shop unless they are the real thing
- Fake pearl necklaces – if the coating has chipped off, there's no saving these
- Enamel jewellery – relics from the seventies
- Bracelets picked up on holiday – and only ever worn on that holiday
- A whole jewellery box – you have had since your teens from which time the contents have become more and more tangled
- The single earring – where is its long lost twin?
- Charm bracelets – the ones with childish souvenirs should be stored away for the next generation
- Watches that don't work any more – if there is no way they can be mended, time to go

WHY KEPT	WHY CHUCK
An heirloom, albeit a fake one	You will never get those missing rhinestones replaced
A Bohemian and fun piece	Could be better in the children's dressing up box
A gorgeous gold necklace	Only plated and it's rubbed off
It's real gold	Sell it
A token of love from an old boyfriend	Your husband might not find it so romantic
My partner bought it for me	It's frumpy – if he asks, say it got lost at the cleaner's

SWIMWEAR

We are talking about two very different items of clothing: the one-piece for swimming, that is not going to slip off as you power through the water, and the bikini, for looking cool and getting a brown tum. If it's cotton, it's better to buy a size too small, as the fabric inevitably stretches when it's wet. And don't leave it until two days before your holiday to buy your swimwear – it will be a miracle if you find something that suits you.

- The navy and white striped one-piece – only good for the pin thin
- The bump-up-your-cleavage, padded, underwired bikini – as long as you fill it, but do not spill out over the top
- The sports swimsuit with go-faster name – this will do NOTHING for your boobs
- The G-string – keep this for the privacy of your back garden
- The fancy strappy contraption – awful for sunbathing
- Shiny, glitzy, gold – were you in the cast of *Dynasty*?

WHY KEPT?	WHY CHUCK?
The bikini top gives me a superb cleavage	So does the bottom, because it's too small
The perfect black sporty one-piece	The fabric has stretched and is now see-through
The underwired top has a wire missing	You'll never wear it again
The top is so pretty	But where is the bottom half?
White really shows off my tan	It looks like dirty underwear

HATS

You are either a hat person or not. If you are like Susannah you'll have dozens of hats that haven't seen daylight for a decade because they are not fit. If you are more like Trinny, you'll have a select and perfect few, that are preserved in hatboxes and forgotten about. Neither of us has stooped as low as the baseball cap.

- The picture hat – because of their size these always end up being stashed away at the top of the wardrobe. The same place acts as a tip for unwanted items or un-foldable clothes that need to be hidden in a flash cleaning frenzy
- The bijoux bonnet – your prettier hats might have become ornaments hanging on an antique hat stand or stacked elegantly in a bedroom corner. Your friends comment on how gorgeous they are. Remember why they are on your wall and not on your head
- The sun hat – probably your oldest friend and the only one you can keep in bad condition. No problem, an old sun hat evokes an air of anti-chic and aristocratic eccentricity
- The baseball cap – have you EVER seen anyone with ANY style sport a baseball cap? Say no more
- The beret and trilby – not in your wildest dreams
- Sporting hats – if they are warm, waterproof and suit you, hang on to them because they are hard to find
- Little woolly winter hats – only suit those with high foreheads

WHY KEPT?	**WHY CHUCK?**
Hats don't come cheap	It's very difficult to get a hat cleaned
It came in its own hatbox	It's still a very eighties hat
I got married in it.	Do you have room for sentimental luxuries?
It's the perfect shape for my face	The ingrained dust does not make it any prettier

SCARVES

Be really honest, how often do you actually wear a scarf, except on cold days and lovebite days? Shawls, especially large soft wool or pashmina ones, are warmer, more versatile and less dated. Unless you are a rich Euro or elegant grandmother, silk squares are for the time being dormant. Give them away to Marie-France and granny.

- School scarf – made of synthetic wool and in rather hideous colours. The regulation fringing, which spent five years dipped in scampi, chips and cider, is now rigid
- The mean velvet scarf – usually in black, brown or a Renaissance colour, it would be terribly useful for the evening if only it was big enough
- The square silk scarf – given by godparents, grandparents and partners, these breed in the cupboard. Elegant on an older lady, frumpy on anyone else
- The wool and 'cashmere' mix – but the cashmere is synthetic angora and doesn't even keep you warm
- The kerchief – the spotted variety, which in its past life was tied around the neck à la cowboy chic. Now used as a hanky and crusty with snot
- The chiffon scarf – so cheap (this being the operative word) they were bought in more than one colour to accessorize all those frumpy floral dresses
- The chenille scarf – a foul fabric that should be burnt
- The fake fur scarf – the only ones worth keeping are those that look so real they have been spat on by Animal Rights activists

WHY KEPT	**WHY CHUCK**
The Hermes type silk scarf	Because you don't need it
It's a lovely colour velvet	It's irreparably marked
So useful in the summer	Doesn't fit around your neck, let alone your shoulders
It's the scarf you wear the most	It shows it
It's cashmere	But yellow was never your colour

GLOVES

It's all too easy to acquire a glut of gloves through impulse purchases and presents from friends. And apart from making sure they fit correctly, no one can say that a glove doesn't suit them. Cull gloves in the summer, when your judgment is not impaired by the possibility of cold hands.

- The woolly hand-warmer – in many colours, none of them matching
- The fur-trimmed friend – seemed a good idea at the time of purchase to add a little zest to the winter coat
- The sad leather glove – hard and shrivelled from getting caught in the rain
- The fashion glove – covered in fringing, feathers, buttons, stitching and basically too much of a good thing
- The sheepskin glove – lovely, warm, cosy but invariably with holes at the fingertips and streaks of snot from wiping nose on cold days
- The stripey glove – no excuse for keeping these
- The mittens – unless you shoot, are an extreme weather artist or are currently in a production of Scrooge, chuck 'em
- The golf glove – essential, we assume, for the lady golfer to protect her hands
- The riding glove – if you ride regularly there will be pairs and singletons dating back to your childhood. They wear out quickly, necessitating frequent updates
- The ski glove – you never think to dry-clean them so the dirt becomes more and more ingrained. This makes them smelly and ready for the bin

WHY KEPT	WHY CHUCK
I bought them in an antique shop	They were always too small
The other one is going to turn up somewhere	Dream on
The most useful colour and fabric	They are beginning to smell very bad
They were really warm	Even since two of your fingers have gone through them?
I've got two of them	But the right one is covered in snot stains from when a hanky wasn't handy

SUMMARY

The culling experience doesn't happen overnight. If you expect to get it over and done with in a matter of hours, you will become frustrated, bad tempered and give up. The best way to handle this exorcism is to set aside a few hours a week until it's done.

Once you have a beautifully streamlined wardrobe, it is important to maintain the quality of its contents by culling at the end of each season. Having done it once it should become second nature. That's the theory, anyway. In our case the reality is that Trinny listens to her own advice while Susannah still wishes she could.

THE TEN COMMANDMENTS

1. You can never throw out too much in your first major cull.
2. Three piles are required: the definitely outs, the maybes and the keeps.
3. A friend will give you the courage to be ruthless.
4. Buy garden refuse bags before the great cull.
5. Pre-buy hangers for prettier hanging, as after the culling there will be gaps in your closet.
6. If you buy the things you love in bulk, chuck the tattiest.
7. Don't forget the accessories and nightgowns.
8. If you have an isolated skirt that you love because it suits you, but have nothing to wear it with, put what you need to make it an outfit on a shopping list.
9. There may be some gorgeous outfits in there that you don't wear because you don't have the right shoes. Buy them.
10. Throw out the maybe pile.

6

GOING SHOPPING

Cindy drives a Sherman tank…

Sherman drives a hard bargain…
koh samui
KAREN MILLEN
ENGLAND
MARILYN
LONDON

INTRODUCTION

Shopping. Retail therapy or purchasing purgatory? Men believe it's a female substitute for sex, but there is no middle ground when it comes to shopping. If you love it, it can either be a full-blown multiple orgasm (Trinny) or a 'wham, bam, thank you ma'am' that leaves you distracted but unsatisfied (Susannah). For some women, however, shopping is utter hell and to be avoided at all costs.

Though we have made our living from shopping, we fully appreciate the anxiety it can cause. Walking into a designer shop filled with snooty assistants takes confidence and guts. Trying on a bikini in an over-lit changing room can turn a poised beauty into an insecure wreck.

Shoving crowds bring out the murderess in even the best-natured woman, while the time it takes to find a basic item in the right style, size and colour can all too easily make us tardy in picking up the kids or in the shit for being late for work again.

Then there is the car issue. Do you take it and risk life for killing the traffic warden or, like a responsible, environmentally caring citizen, do you catch the bus and then have to spend a fortune with the osteopath having defiantly taken on the role of pack horse?

All the above factors contribute to an unhappy experience, mistake purchases and wasted money. Trousers that are too tight but bought with the intention of losing weight. A bland skirt paid for out of frustration at not having the time to find the one you really want. Fuchsia shoes that are too small but bought anyway because they were the only pair suitable for the party that night.

Parking tickets, wheelclamps, bad backs, sore feet, overdrafts and unwanted items can all be avoided once you understand that shopping is an art. There are rules and regulations, which if followed will turn the shopaholic into a restrained buyer and the phobic into an assured shopper who knows exactly what she wants.

SUSANNAH'S TOP TIPS

- Because my tits are a size bigger than my bottom, I will always take in a bikini in a size twelve and fourteen. I simply swap the tops in the changing room to get the perfect size swimwear. I know there are an equal number of women out there whose bums are bigger than their busts. One day, shops will learn to offer the choice.
- Make a complaint if a sales assistant is rude – You'll leave the shop feeling better and you won't be put off going back there.
- Do go over budget if you find something that really suits you – you won't regret it.

'Even if it's minus 20, don't wear layers of clothes; you'll only get hot and bothered in the stores and exhausted from having to put on and take off so many items. This will shorten your quest and you will end up buying either nothing or something that will need culling in the next streamlining session'

'Don't forget parking meter money – it's no good getting a bargain and coming back to a £30 parking fine'

'If you take a partner because you want him to pay, make sure you have identified what you are after before you set off. Any hanging around will render him pissed off and sulky. If you are considering taking him along for advice, forget it. He's not interested'

'Pop socks are a disaster if you are looking for dresses or skirts. If you leave them on you will be put off buying anything and if you take them off they leave a hideous tide mark at the fattest part of your calf'

'If you are used to wearing make-up at night and are in search of an evening look, don't venture down the high street bare-faced. Your naked blemishes will not do the outfit any justice'

'Don't stuff your face with food before you go shopping – your stomach will bloat and you will feel like shit about your body'

'Don't take your credit cards out with you if you are overdrawn and know you might spend more than the limit on the card'

'Don't wear ugly underwear as you will get no respect from shop assistants'

'Don't wear boots as they are a bugger to get on and off, and often cause unsightly swelling after too much pavement surfing'

TRINNY'S TOP TIPS

• Always check the rear view when trying on clothes.
• If the changing room has distorting mirrors, the closer you are, the more realistic the image.
• Do pay proportionately for how often the item will be worn. You'll feel better spending a couple of hundred pounds on a coat for everyday than an evening top you wear four times a year.
• Do pay more for classics and less for fads.

'Don't rely on paying for chewing gum with a large note to get coins for the parking meter. Vendors are wise to this so take your own supply'

'Do make sure you are wearing the right bra when buying tops. An exercise bap holder will do nothing for a pretty camisole. If you are in a department store and in need of support, borrow one'

'A light lunch and hence a flatter stomach will make you feel better about your body and more inclined to find the perfect something'

'Take a pair of high-heeled shoes when searching for a cocktail dress or anything else that may require extra height'

'Take a bag that hangs across you, eliminating the need to carry more than you have to'

'Make a list of what is lacking in your wardrobe and outfits you never seem to have enough of (e.g. everyday tops), as well as anything specific you are after'

'Feet get tired at the best of times, so comfortable shoes are of primary importance'

CAN'T AFFORD TO SHOP BUT NEED A FIX

INTRODUCTION

Why is it that when we are in a rush, all our nice clothes seem to hide at the back of the cupboard? The shirt that goes with your favourite suit is nowhere to be seen and the taximeter is ticking outside. Your husband is yelling at you to get a flipping move on, and you've got nothing to wear. You're doomed to wearing the same black outfit again.

You'd love to go on a spending spree to alleviate the problem but this would mean dipping into the housekeeping cash.

The reason your wardrobe is bare, yet bulging at the seams, is because garments are divided into separates. We all do it. Trousers huddle in one corner, shirts in another, while jackets and coats ancestrally share wire hangers that struggle to take the strain.

This pseudo organization results in chaos. The explanation? When it comes to getting dressed, you still have to pull these pieces together into outfits and this always takes more time than you think. The outcome is combinations that lack imagination.

To utilize your clothes effectively requires taking time out to create ready-hung outfits. This works especially well with colour. Your basic blacks and whites can remain grouped together in their usual habitat, but the colourful clothes can be re-arranged according to complementary shade, tone, texture and fabric. By doing this you will find that a paisley top you've hardly worn looks fantastic with a velvet coat you use every day, or transforms a skirt that you're bored with into a fab new outfit.

HANGING

Hanging clothes in an efficient way will make your life easier. The contents of your wardrobe will look neater and free from chaos. We hang as much as possible because shoving something back on a hanger takes less time than folding. Clothes crease less and last longer.

Whenever you are feeling the pinch, but have some spare time, change around your hanging order so clothes get to know one other better. Re-introduce old friends, allow them to make new ones. Never again will you have to spend so much money.

- Dresses – make a cheap dress look more expensive by putting it on a nice velvet hanger. Superficial but effective
- Trousers – where possible hang trousers straight from their hem: this prevents creasing and eases the ironing load
- Don't ever pile trousers on top of each other on one hanger, or the bottom pair will disappear
- Shirts – try hanging them all on hangers from one shop that you go to a lot. This gives continuity and is a must for the super-anally retentive
- Hidden friends – if you are a lover of camisoles, try hanging them next to complementary coloured cardigans, where they have a chance of being shown off. If you fold them with your T-shirts, they will remain unworn
- Take some of your favourite jumpers that you haven't worn for a while and try hanging them next to a skirt or trousers of a similar or complementary colour
- Outfits – hang clothes in complete outfits whenever possible
- Fabrics – it's best to mix fabrics in outfits. All velvet,for example, is too much of a good thing. With cotton, try to mix textures
- Neutral colours – black, white and taupe basics should be hung in their separate categories (jackets, trousers, skirts) rather than being mixed together
- Colour – group all your clothes by shade, then hang these shades next to similar colours e.g. yellow-orange-red-maroon-pink. Or put blues with purples, next to greys

TOOLS

- Padded hangers – preferably in velvet – so dresses don't slip
- Short clip hangers – for trousers to be hung by hem
- Long clip hangers – for skirts to be hung by waist
- Wooden hangers – for coats and jackets
- Freebie hangers – OK as long as they are wood or plastic
- Discard wire hangers immediately as they make clothes look cheap, promote creases like a virus and are best used for breaking into cars
- Hanging lavender bags – for added luxury

- Belts – never put belts in drawers. They will get muddled and you won't be able to open the drawer. Hang them on tie racks or over the hook of a hanger

SHELVES AND FOLDING

JERSEYS

- Put jumpers in colour ranges, with dark tones at the bottom grading up to lighter ones at the top
- Don't make high piles as they will topple, dumping favourite items at the back of the shelf
- Don't keep folding away dirty jumpers. There is nothing a moth loves more than feasting on spilt egg or ground-in chocolate
- In the summer, put away big jumpers – dry-cleaned and well-folded – into plastic bags. When winter comes round and you take them out they will feel like a new purchase

T-SHIRTS AND SWEATS

- Leave a gap in between each pile – you might have to fold them into smaller shapes but it will keep shelves tidier for longer
- The tops and bottoms of casual sweats and sports clothes should always be folded next to each other so you won't need to spend ages finding partners

SCARVES

- Fold scarves (wool, cashmere and silk) next to sweaters of a similar colour; you will remember to wear them more often

JEANS

- Crunched jeans are far cooler than precisely ironed ones, so it's fine to fold them

TOOLS

- Cinnamon sticks, or cloves, to ward off moths
- Lavender bags for aroma
- Plastic bags (use old dry-cleaning covers)
- Lining paper

DRAWERS

Drawers are for the smaller items in your wardrobe and they become untidy faster than any other section. It's easy to close a drawer to the world, which means that during rush hour underwear can be slung in haphazardly, only to be swallowed in a quicksand of pop socks. Bras, knickers, socks and tights create a melting pot of confusion as they get mixed up and lose their identity.

To get your drawers organized, never pile items on top of each other. Pack them in rows like books in a flat bookshelf.

TOOLS

- Luxurious lining paper
- Lavender bags, so it all smells great
- Dividers – either shoe boxes or cardboard/plastic dividers

UNDERWEAR

- Buy plastic dividers for knickers and bras or, if your drawers are deep enough, put in old shoeboxes (without the lid!)
- Divide knickers by both colour and style, because if a nude G-string is running riot among the flesh-coloured granny knickers, you'll never find it
- Divide bras into categories: everyday, sports, evening dress

TIGHTS AND POP SOCKS

- Separate tights from pop socks and hold-ups or stockings
- Never put back tights or pop socks with holes or runs
- If you keep holey tights to wear under long skirts, confine them to a plastic bag
- Separate black, navy and dark brown tights in a good light, so that you don't get it wrong in a bleary morning rush
- Expensive tights last longer if they are kept in their original packaging, to differentiate them from their everyday cousins

SOCKS

- Segregate by warmth factor and sport, e.g. cotton, wool, cashmere; gym, tennis, walking, shooting

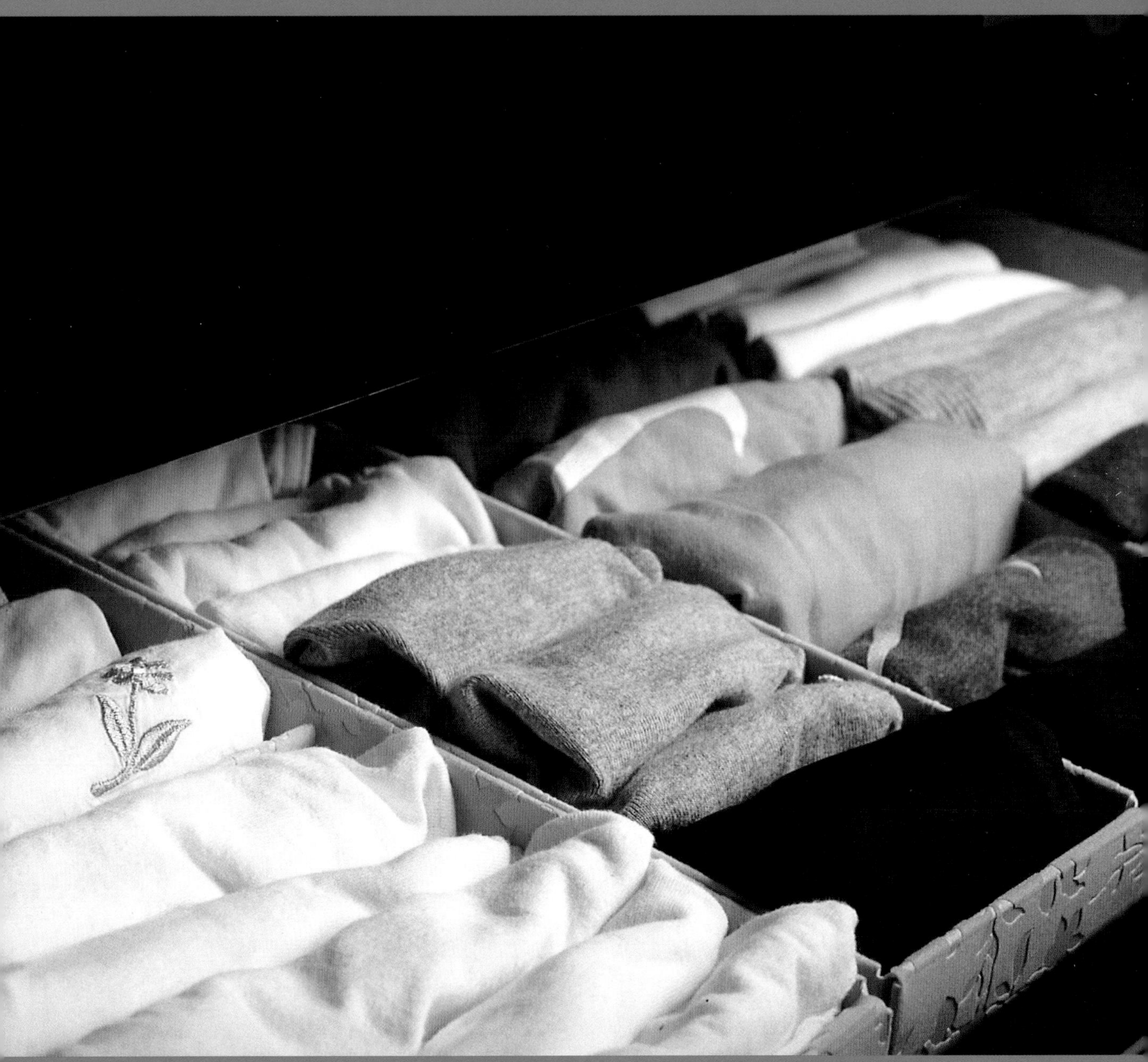

SHOE BOXES

The area of one's cupboard that most resembles a jumble sale is the shoe department. If they are always piled on top of each other in an orgy of disarray, our shoes don't stand a chance. Give the poor guys a break with a new home that is orderly and un-cramped. They'll serve you much better and last a whole lot longer.

NEW SHOES
Don't be afraid to wear a pair of expensive new shoes – you didn't buy them just so they could sit in their box until they begin to look dated. Besides which, shoes last better if worn in rotation rather than wearing the same few pairs day after day.

EVENING SHOES
Keep evening shoes in their boxes. Take a Polaroid or just an ordinary photograph of each pair and stick it on the box so they are readily identifiable.

TRAINERS
Relegate smelly trainers to solitary confinement.

WET SHOES
Put them in a cool, dry place, stuffed with newspaper, until they are completely dry.

CLEANING
This should be obvious, but get all your shoes and boots and give them a good polish. You will make discoveries that appear far more wearable after their brush up.

SHOETREES
How many pairs of shoes do you own that cost a pretty packet but you never wear because they have lost their shape? Buy shoetrees and, more importantly, use them.

TOOLS

- Keep all shoe boxes If you have the room
- Camera for identification pix
- Shoetrees: cedar wood for flat shoes that tend to smell; plastic for court shoes
- Plastic toe trees for mules and slingbacks
- A good cleaning kit – that you use

SWAPPING

There was a time when we always shopped together. It was more fun and helpful to have each other's advice on what to buy. The strange thing was that we only wore a small proportion of the items we bought. It took a while to realize that what we had recommended to each other were in fact the things we inherently knew should be in our own closets. A swapping session ensued and this is an example of two such outfits.

SUSANNAH'S MISTAKES

- Tight dress squidges boobs to the side, making her waist disappear
- Double chin is shown off to the maximum effect by the high neckline
- Why cover a great cleavage?
- It's no use trying to hide those arms, they still look flabby
- Her voluptuous body shape makes sequins look cheap and tarty
- Geometric pattern widens the soft roundness of her body
- The shoes look clumsy and inelegant on her fine ankles

TRINNY'S MISTAKES

- An over-exposed neckline makes her look scrawny
- Her boobs nowhere near fill the bodice
- She shouldn't hide her stunning sculpted arms
- A bell shaped skirt does nothing to thin down her thighs
- The hem of the skirt draws attention to the widest part of her calf
- The clothes hang unflatteringly off her slim frame, making the outfit look drab
- Slingbacks just make her thick ankles look thicker

TIPS

- Make a list of the friends you have shopped with the most
- Call them and ask what they don't wear in their wardrobe
- Have a swapping session
- Learn from your mistakes – shop with them again but don't take their advice
- If you're recommending something for someone else – maybe you should try it on yourself

TRINNY IN SUSANNAH'S CLOTHES

- By showing off her arms she looks more sophisticated
- The high neckline takes away the need for bosoms
- The diamond pattern compliments her angular shoulders
- Her defined sharp shape makes the sequins look classy
- A wall of fabric hides the point her ass ends, making her legs appear longer
- The hem catches her leg at its narrowest point
- The heels don't look as if they are going to snap under the weight of her calves

SUSANNAH IN TRINNY'S CLOTHES

- The bodice winches in her waist
- And its low neckline draws attention to her ample breasts
- The cardigan covers her giant upper arms
- And ends in the middle of her tummy hiding it just enough
- A three-quarter length sleeve draws the eye to her slim wrists
- The skirt length hides her baggy knees
- A skirt cut on the bias clings to her legs, her best feature
- Because she has small ankles she can wear slingbacks, which make her legs look even longer

NEW FRIENDS FROM OLD ACQUAINTANCES

In the world of the Waltons and Little House on the Prairie, clothes get mended. John Boy's life is part of a cottage industry where domestic functions are alive and well. In our modern and less idyllic world the idea of darning a sock or hooking an eye is an anathema. We have 'far more important' things to do like shop and look gorgeous. With this in mind and the dream world of quilt-making behind us, here follows our updated version of smocking and lace-making.

SKIRTS

Problem	Solution
Zip broken	Either throw it away – it can't be a favourite if it's taking so long to fix – or take it to a good dry-cleaners and get it repaired
Hem come down	*Temporary* – safety pin, super glue, double-sided tape *Permanent* – take it to the menders or do it yourself
Too short to wear	Put velvet trim or brocade around the bottom

TROUSERS

Problem	Solution
Jeans with knee gone	Cut off for sexy frayed shorts
Hem down	*Temporary* – take down totally, iron out crease and wear high heels or cut off as above. *Permanent* – go to the menders or sew it yourself
Too tight at top	Wear with skirt over – if it's your style
White trousers with visible pockets	Cut them out – and sew up the hole if you have a habit of putting loose change in your pocket

DRESSES

Problem	Solution
A long dress you never wear	If you still like the top, chop off the bottom and wear it as a top
Frumpy, unflattering length	Take it up to a length that flatters your legs. Will make a dramatic difference

SHIRTS

Problem	Solution
Unfitted but great colour	Don't use the buttons, simply knot the bottom
Good shape, boring colour	Dye it

JUMPERS

Problem	Solution
Good shape, wrong colour	If cashmere, have it professionally dyed; otherwise dye in the washing machine
Boring cardigan	Trim with ribbon, beads or brocade
Cashmere which has lost its softness	This will have been dry-cleaned just one too many times. Hand wash it with soap flakes and a conditioner and roll dry in a towel

COATS AND JACKETS

Problem	Solution
Favourite coat you no longer wear	Put a fur trim on collar, cuffs or hem to give a new lease of life
Wide lapels that don't suit you	Can easily be taken in by a good mender
Button off	In an emergency, fasten through from the back with safety pin
Cheap buttons	Swap for beautiful bone ones. They will also make a cheap coat look expensive
Pregnant so nothing fits	Wear your usual coat (single-breasted), but don't attempt to do it up. Wear a long scarf in front to cover the gap

SHOES

Problem	Solution
Ankle straps that don't suit you	Cut off the ankle strap and they will become new, different shoes
Dated colour	Dye them in a darker colour and you'll get loads more wear out of them

STORAGE

Finding and creating imaginative storage methods is immensely beneficial. It relieves bulging cupboards and frees up space so that you can live without climbing over mountains of clothes or rummaging through unpacked suitcases. We never seemed to have enough wardrobe space – until now. Read on and ring the changes in your hoarding habits.

- Never store anything dirty
- If you don't have much room, find drawers that go under your bed or a bed with drawers
- If you haven't got enough drawers, put suitcases under beds for storing clothes
- Put away summer shoes in winter
- Store slim evening bags with straps by hanging them on nails inside your cupboard doors
- Hang necklaces and bracelets next to evening bags in the same colours on the inside of cupboard doors – and transform that little black dress into a stylish evening outfit
- Store hats inside each other in hat boxes, with newspaper in each rim
- Store empty suitcases inside each other

SUMMARY

Shopping is fun and addictive, but what is much more satisfying is realizing that you don't need to go on a manic spending spree to get yourself a whole new look. Yes, you will probably need a few special little items that make you an original dresser, but the desperate urge to bulk buy will be dramatically reduced once you have fixed the physical layout of your wardrobe and found new friends among your old acquaintances.

THE TEN COMMANDMENTS

1. Give your wardrobe a good workout – it's twice as satisfying as a day shopping.
2. Buy the right hangers for trousers, skirts and dresses.
3. Hang coloured clothes together as outfits.
4. Keep stacked piles narrow for neatness and visibility.
5. Divide underwear by colour and style: day, sport, night.
6. Polish up old shoes for a new lease of life.
7. Buy shoetrees – and use them.
8. Invite a shopping pal for a bit of clothes swapping, then do the same at her house.
9. Always put your clothes away at night.
10. Keep it all tidy – it will only work if you can find it.

8

HOW TO DRESS FOR YOUR PERSONALITY AND LIFESTYLE

The sooner we get
our just desserts
the better

INTRODUCTION

There are numerous occasions in life when meticulous dress planning is required. Your instinct will lead you to pick up the phone to your best friend. Don't listen to her. What is right for her will almost certainly be wrong for you.

The most important aspect of dressing for your personality and lifestyle is to be true to yourself, reflecting your character in what you wear while taking into account whom you will be meeting.

No matter how much you want to impress someone, wearing clothes that aren't really you will send out all sorts of wrong messages. For example, if you're meeting the in-laws for the first time, looking rich will create barriers within your future family. Overdoing it when meeting your husband's ex-wife will give her the satisfaction of knowing that insecurity has led you to try too hard.

But equally, whatever anyone says, first impressions make an impact. Yes, when you walk into the headmistress's office dressed like a slut, clever conversation can change her opinion, but why not get it right from the start?

Though we stress it's best to dress for the situation we are not suggesting you dress inappropriately for your lifestyle. The lady who lunches doesn't have to swap her designer shoes for the country, just wear flat plain ones as opposed to glitzy Manolo's.

In this chapter we have chosen examples of scenarios we feel most of you will identify with. There are sketches for mums with young babies and advice for the uptight to chill out. Bigger and older women can see how easy it is to look sexy, while younger, slimmer women can learn that an expensive label doesn't always attract the right type of man.

NORMANDY – RELAX, IT'S SATURDAY

A chilled day for Normandy involves making herself even more perfect at the hairdresser and beauty salon before she heads out for a 'casual' lunch with girlfriends. Her attire is all beautifully cut and outstandingly costly. She needs to understand that this continuous level of upkeep makes her appear cheap rather than expensive. If she didn't work so hard on her appearance she would be more approachable – she has to let go of being perfect.

WHY SHE CHOSE THE WRONG OUTFIT

- Fur trimmed designer cardigan. It was on the cover of *Vogue* – but she's inviting competition with her girlfriends
- Italian cut trousers. She feels safe in a tailored look that is recognizable by its designer name. They are too structured for a chilled out Saturday
- Black high-heeled suede boots – bought to go with the trousers, so they make her look even smarter
- Huge real rock on finger – insecurity doesn't let her take it off. But it's too flash and maybe some of her friends aren't so well off
- Perfect make-up – it's her armour. She doesn't need it to look pretty
- The overall message is of an insecure person, who feels she will be judged by how she dresses

THE RIGHT WAY AND WHY IT WORKS

- Bootleg trousers – the shape is fab for flat shoes
- White T-shirt – immediate relaxed Saturday feel
- Deep V-neck cashmere – luxurious material that is bland enough not to shriek 'designer'
- Small diamond cross – discreet bit of flashiness

DRESSING TO PULL

Normandy is always on the lookout for a hunk. Tonight could be her night as she's going out to a smart dinner and knows that there will be a plethora of sexy single men. Of course she has to make a special effort to look gorgeous, but if she's not careful she will attract the wrong sort of man.

WHY SHE CHOSE THE WRONG OUTFIT

- Loud, patterned, deep V-neck dress. She thinks no one will speak to her if she doesn't show off her tits – but nice men like a bit of mystery
- Sequinned sandals. They give her confidence because of their height, but she can't dance in them
- Sparkly dangly earrings, for a touch of glamour; they're too loud, too trashy, too Tramp nightclub
- The message coming across loud and clear is: 'too hot to handle'. Will attract the kind of man who thinks he's a stud and needs a trophy girlfriend

THE RIGHT WAY AND WHY IT WORKS

- Silver dress – still showing off cleavage, but it's covert not overt
- Silver sandals – high enough to make legs look good, so who cares if she can't dancc in thcm?
- Hair and make-up – gives her a Mia Farrow vulnerability, with enough confidence to look natural
- Antique paste jewellery makes her look well bred and classy
- This look shows off her female sensuality while allowing men to see the real her

LORNA – SCHOOL SPORTS DAY

It's her son's sports day, but for Lorna the competition is less about the track, more about the other mothers in the field. Getting her daughter ready and the picnic organized and picking up hubby from work en route doesn't leave her time to think about what she will wear. She knows the outfit must be comfortable enough to win the egg and spoon race and that skirts are out when eating on the floor.

WHY SHE CHOSE THE WRONG OUTFIT

- Jeans. For running around all day, plus she didn't have time to change. Slovenly
- Jumper around waist. She thinks it hides her bottom, but it's winching in a baggy T-shirt and the colour cuts her in half. And it's too casual
- Big T-shirt. It's her daily look, and she feels comfortable. You know our thoughts on big T-shirts
- Trainers. Good for running. But it's not the winning that's important, it's looking smart while taking part that counts
- She looks like a mother who can't be bothered to make an effort

THE RIGHT WAY AND WHY IT WORKS

- Wide leg pedal pushers – a bit trendy, to impress her children's precociously fashion-conscious friends
- Rather tight camisole dress – it's sexy for dad, cool for kids and light for a hot summer day
- Cardy around waist – arranged to camouflage her bum rather than give her a waist
- Miu Miu shoe – her individuality on show, and she won't be tempted to run – most uncool
- Here's a mother who doesn't spend time making an effort to look fab – it comes naturally (if only they knew!)

SEDUCING YOUR HUSBAND

She knows her husband feels she has let herself go, and they never seem to go out any more, so she has decided to prepare a romantic diner à deux. They haven't had sex in months, so she wants to seduce him into bed afterwards. Will there or won't there be a third baby on the way?

WHY SHE CHOSE THE WRONG OUTFIT

- Negligee. He found it sexy on their honeymoon – but she'll look stupid serving dinner in it
- Fluffy mules. No other footwear would go with the negligee.You need a house full of servants to wear fluffy mules
- Flowers in hair for extra femininity. They'll poke his eye out mid-snog
- The whole look brings pudding to the first course. Penetration before the foreplay. Too much too soon

THE RIGHT WAY AND WHY IT WORKS

- Bare feet – he knows it's her erogenous zone
- Low cut silk dress – tits on show in privacy of their own home
- Cashmere cardigan – sensual to the touch and coverage for her fat arms
- The message conveyed here is that having dinner at home is as special as going out

TRINNY – A COUNTRY WALK

Trinny has been invited to the country, a place she is not overly familiar with. She has been forewarned that the weather is unpredictable and that long walks will be a part of the entertainment. This is cool, she has a dog, she's done Hyde Park and knows the dirt implications of having to rub down a wet pet. Does she appreciate a ploughed field? We'll find out.

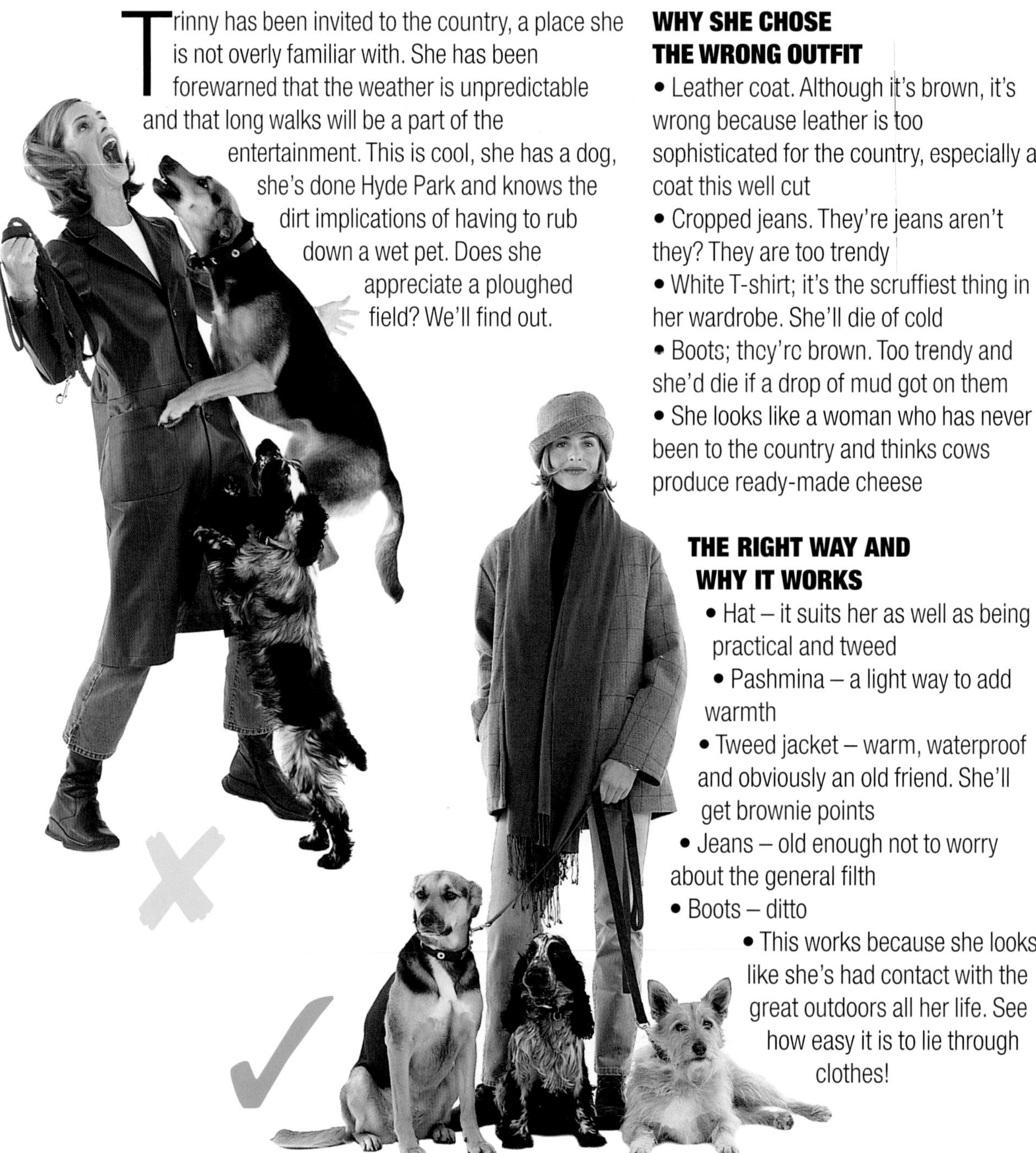

WHY SHE CHOSE THE WRONG OUTFIT

- Leather coat. Although it's brown, it's wrong because leather is too sophisticated for the country, especially a coat this well cut
- Cropped jeans. They're jeans aren't they? They are too trendy
- White T-shirt; it's the scruffiest thing in her wardrobe. She'll die of cold
- Boots; they're brown. Too trendy and she'd die if a drop of mud got on them
- She looks like a woman who has never been to the country and thinks cows produce ready-made cheese

THE RIGHT WAY AND WHY IT WORKS

- Hat – it suits her as well as being practical and tweed
- Pashmina – a light way to add warmth
- Tweed jacket – warm, waterproof and obviously an old friend. She'll get brownie points
- Jeans – old enough not to worry about the general filth
- Boots – ditto
- This works because she looks like she's had contact with the great outdoors all her life. See how easy it is to lie through clothes!

MEETING THE IN-LAWS

Meeting the in-laws took a long time in coming for Trinny. Her fiancé was nervous at the prospect (typical man) and kept stalling the event. This procrastination turned a potentially happy meeting into a major summit. Trinny knew she had only one shot at this. They would either love or loathe her first time around.

WHY SHE CHOSE THE WRONG OUTFIT

- Pink top. Chosen for its flattering colour, but it's too loud and ostentatious
- Grey skirt – to flatter her legs. Too sexy for mother-in-law
- High shoes – to make legs look longer. Her father-in-law might be 5 foot 3
- Bare legs to show off tan. A bit disrespectful to bare naked flesh
- Heavy make-up to cover a late night. Where's the fresh-faced virgin?
- Hair – she felt a trip to the hairdresser was necessary. Trying too hard
- First impression? She's, er, great fun…for a mistress

THE RIGHT WAY AND WHY IT WORKS

- Outfit shows off her individuality and confidence with her style. The colours are warm and inviting, while retaining sophistication
- Shoes – flat enough for comfort and approachability
- Make-up – makes her look like a natural beauty (ho! ho!)
- Hair – she's handy with a hair dryer
- Jewellery – necklaces are Trinny"s signature accessory and a talking point
- She looks like a confident, independent girl who will be a worthy wife for their son

SUSANNAH - TRAVELLING ON A PLANE

Before Susannah had baby Joe, the first priority when travelling was a smart comfortable outfit to facilitate the possibility of an upgrade. As any mother knows, young baby + travel + nice clothes = vomit, soggy biscuits, no upgrade and a large dry-cleaning bill. Looking cool while fending off dribble and sick is a challenge that must be met before S and J's flight to the States.

WHY SHE CHOSE THE WRONG OUTFIT

- Silken designer coat. It doesn't crease – but it attracts and holds vomit like a magnet
- Velvet palazzo pants. So comfortable – but velvet marks more easily than any other fabric
- Boots. They zip on and off and are flat and comfortable – but they won't bc comfy or easy to get back on once your feet have swollen

THE RIGHT WAY AND WHY IT WORKS

- Leather jacket – sick wipes off with an easy swipe
- Necklace – feminine and also something for Joe to play with in the queue
- Trousers – non-crease, machine-washable wool
- Shoes – flat, comfy, with plenty of room for enlargement
- Jersey around the waist – cashmere for warmth and luxury and it's out of the biscuit zone
- I qualify for an upgrade

MEETING YOUR MAN'S EX

Now Susannah is happily married, there is no earthly reason why she should have a problem hooking up with her husband's first love. She is having a party at her home, where she will have the advantage of being the centre of attention. Ridiculous though it is, Susannah feels a nervous jealousy she cannot control. She must look sexy, successful, beautiful, thin, tall and blissfully happy.

WHY SHE CHOSE THE WRONG OUTFIT

- Brown dress. Sexy shape, but drab for a party
- Fishnet tights, for a sexy look. Trying too hard
- High strappy sandals – because the ex is 5 foot 4. After too much to drink she could fall over
- Loads of make-up. A protective shield. She looks unapproachable and scary
- Hair feathers, to be original. Actually, a bit too subtle

THE RIGHT WAY AND WHY IT WORKS

- Outfit says: 'I'm here, you can't miss me, and I'm confident enough to wear a cheap sweater with a sarong that's 15 years old and still carry it off'
- Shoes. Second-hand shoes are unique, distinguishing her from all the other girls in designer heels
- Jewellery – using flowers to look pretty rather than diamonds to look like she has a generous husband
- Make-up gives a healthy glow that belies the fact she's older than the ex
- Hair – sleek and chic

JOANNA – LUNCH IN A COUNTRY PUB

At last it's happened; her MD has asked her out. They are off for a romantic lunch at a pub in the country. He loves the countryside so she must show that she is as at home behind a haystack as she is behind her desk.

WHY SHE CHOSE THE WRONG OUTFIT

- Tweed suit. She thinks it's very county set, but it's too stiff, too smart, too un-shaggable
- Flat brogues. Good for walking. Very Margaret Rutherford
- Large handbag. Fits in a clean outfit for next day. She shouldn't sleep with him on the first date

THE RIGHT WAY AND WHY IT WORKS

- Polo neck jumper – makes her fake tits look natural and hides her lack of chin
- Long wool blanket skirt – figure-hugging enough to make him want to look more closely at what is underneath
- High-heeled brown suede boots – these boots aren't made for walking but they do make her legs appear longer
- Subtle earrings, but no other jewellery. He might take the hint and buy her some

MIXING BUSINESS WITH PLEASURE

The lunch went so well, he's asked her to go to his best friend's 50th birthday party. There will be 200 people attending, of whom she will only know her direct boss. Unfortunately her boss fancies the MD as well. Joanna doesn't want her to find out about this budding romance.

WHY SHE CHOSE THE WRONG OUTFIT

- Black trouser suit. Discreet, yet desirable. Wrong: it's too corporate. Get feminine, girl
- High heels, to make her legs longer. High heels with a trouser suit – yuk
- The bag. Goes with the trouser suit. Too like a briefcase. Does she ever give up on work?
- The pendant – a talking piece. It's too long – does she want people to talk to her navel?

THE RIGHT WAY AND WHY IT WORKS

- Velvet dress. She looks pretty and feminine
- Choker. Now this is a really unusual piece. It also hides that lack of chin and emphasizes her long neck
- Mid-heeled mules – could be higher but the colour is perfect for the dress
- Beaded bag. Cute and part of the outfit
- She's made a special effort for the MD and maybe her direct boss won't recognize her because she looks so different from work

ROSEMARY – SUNDAY LUNCH

Rosemary loves giving Sunday lunches – in fact she's become quite well known for them. Friends look forward to her excellent cooking and eclectic choice of wines. She always likes to dress up for these occasions, but this week she needs to make an extra effort as her old school friend and rival is coming. They haven't seen each other for 30 years and Rosemary is sure she will have aged more than Anne.

WHY SHE CHOSE THE WRONG OUTFIT

- Loose tunic. Chosen for comfort and because it has the appearance of having not made too much of an effort. It's an appalling colour for grey hair and she looks as if she's made no effort at all
- Loose pale trousers – part of the outfit. Too much of a bad thing. The shape is fine, but the whole look is dowdy
- She looks like a woman weighed down by life and lack of it

THE RIGHT WAY AND WHY IT WORKS

- The wrap dress is colourful, groovy as opposed to trendy, easy to put on and not too warm for central heating. The narrow velvet palazzo pants give richness
- Shoes – flat and comfy but with a wedge heel to give a bit of height
- Cheap, fun, plastic amber necklace
- Make-up – moisturizing but shine-free
- Hair – done the day before so she feels smart and confident

A FORMAL DINNER

Rosemary is off with her husband to a black tie dinner. She won't know many people there, so has no relevant friends she can ring for advice about what to wear. She would love to slip into an old friend but feels it's time to splash out on something new. She wants to make her husband feel proud of his glamorous wife. What the hell should she get to look alluring while maintaining her dignity?

WHY SHE CHOSE THE WRONG OUTFIT

- Silk kaftan. It's comfortable, and her husband bought it on a business trip to Greece. How unsophisticated: an unflattering piece of cloth that's only good for covering sunburnt skin on holiday
- Bronze beaded bag. The nearest thing she possesses to an evening bag. It bears no relation to the sack she is wearing
- Sixties' gold sandals. Nice and flat yet perfect for the evening. These are fabulous – but not with a kaftan
- The belt. It's part of the kaftan – but it makes her waist look even bigger
- What does this outfit convey? Here's an old woman who doesn't have the inclination to shop any more

THE RIGHT WAY AND WHY IT WORKS

- Choker – marks her out as an individual and stylish dresser
- Coat – this isn't as formal as a dress but, boy, is it elegant. It gives her a waist without squeezing the life out of her
- Trousers – risqué but dead cool
- Mules – more comfortable and less aging than sandals
- A woman who isn't scared of getting old, with a sense of fun and deep-rooted allure. She was obviously a tremendous beauty in her youth

SUMMARY

Like the women types represented in this book, the situations we have placed them in are stereotypes. They are there as examples from which you can adapt your own solutions to dressing for momentous or monotonous occasions in your own life. Wearing the correct type of clothes will help you fit in – adding your own sense of style will make you stand out from the crowd. Being appropriately dressed will help you get what you want and give you the confidence to be relaxed while doing so. Have a good time, girls!

THE TEN COMMANDMENTS

1. Remember, you may not have been born with style – but you can create it.
2. Take into account the occasion and the people you are sharing it with before you dress.
3. Choose an accessory to make your own – be it bags or bracelets.
4. Don't be scared of appearing different from your friends.
5. You will feel more comfortable if you are under-dressed rather than overdressed – and you will intimidate others less.
6. Subtle is sexy – vulgar is not.
7. If you can't walk in your high heels, they won't give you confidence.
8. Friends may be rude about your new-found style – it's only because they are jealous.
9. Even if you are only nipping to the shops, it doesn't mean you have to be without style – you can make your most basic sweatpant story stylish.
10. If you are a dog owner – wear a nicked hairdressing gown to drive to parties in and avoid arriving hair-laden.

9
REPLACING YOUR WARDROBE WITH A SUITCASE

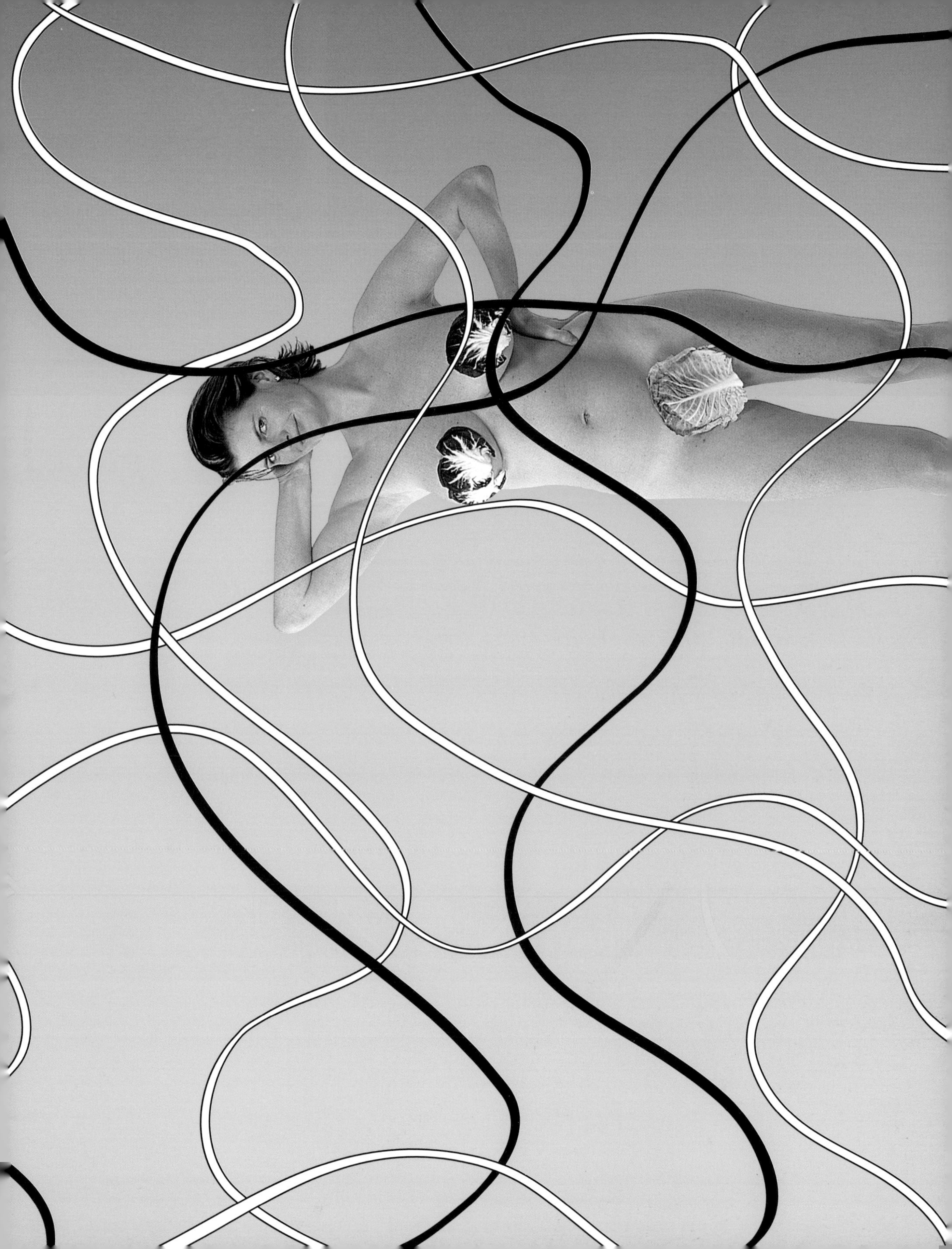

INTRODUCTION

If you are like Susannah, leaving home for a trip creates havoc, causes palpitations and wipes out entire forests with the amount of lists she makes. She begins thinking about what to take at least a month before and will pack the contents of her suitcase in an empty drawer two weeks before departure. Trinny is quite and most annoyingly different.

Already late for her train, plane or automobile, she is able to whip up a delicious concoction of retail recipes in a flash. Her idea of planning is pulling down the suitcase and miraculously chucking in the perfect selection of clothes for her destination. Even more irritating, the contents will arrive crease- and leaked cleanser-free, while Susannah will have to send some pieces to the dry-cleaners and most will need a good pressing.

Now, we represent extreme ends of the spectrum. Everyone would love to have Trinny's talent, but this comes from years of jet-setting and leaping on trains at a moment's notice. Susannah, though not as experienced, does have a method to her madness – so a combination of the two should provide the ideal balance.

A common error made by all women is that we take too much. Partners roll their eyes and inquire whether we have included the proverbial kitchen sink as we drag a trunk downstairs. It's always a question of carting everything 'just in case'.

A refined selection that covers every eventuality is your goal. This is easier than it sounds. Why? Well, holiday clothes need not be fashionable clothes. We find that our travelling wardrobes have hardly changed at all over the past five years. This is because each time we have ventured onto foreign soil – be it for business, sex, or leisure – we have made a note of what we took versus what we actually wore.

DIRTY WEEKEND

A weekend away to indulge in carnal pursuits is one time when the very essence of enjoyment involves no clothes at all. Of course, you will not be arriving at your destination and dining naked, but all you need are your very favourite clothes – as long as they are easy to slip out of and are not tight at any point, otherwise they will leave red marks on your body.

This is not to say that you only need a toothbrush – and don't forget a light cleanser to whisk away panda eyes. Items that help create an atmosphere of seduction should make up the contents of a small overnight bag.

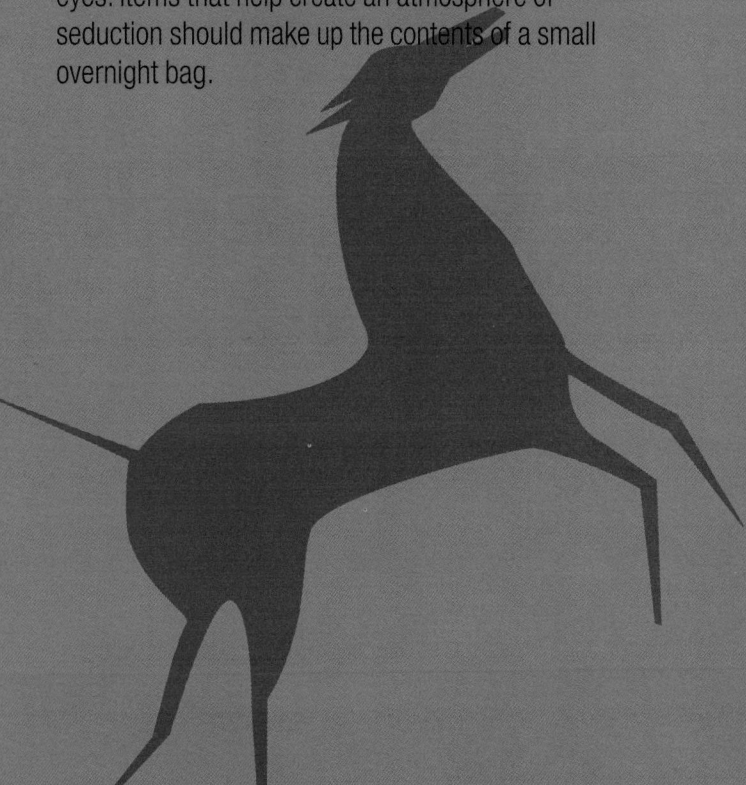

CONTENTS

SEXY UNDERWEAR
A given.
SCENTED CANDLE
There is nothing like candlelight to flatter skin tones and one that smells like heaven is a bonus.
CHAMPAGNE
The price of alcohol is always astronomical in hotels so take your own to break down inhibitions by getting lightly smashed.
MASSAGE OIL
Get to work on those erogenous zones.
EROTICA
Be it in book or video format, a little light porn never hurts.
EXFOLIATOR AND BODY LOTION
Smooth skin will go a long way towards getting a rousing ride from your lover.
AROMATHERAPY BATH/SHOWER GEL
To re-energize – together, of course.

CRABTREE
& EVELYN
La Source
GEL
SHOWER GEL
GEL DOUCHE
PATRICK SÜSKIND
Perfume
CHAMPAGNE
BRUT
BRUT
CHAMPAGNE
Charles LEPRINCE
GRANDE RESERVE
THE BODY SHOP
AROMATHERAPY
ENERGIZING
Body Oil
FOR BATH, BODY & MASSAGE
4.2 FL OZ (125 mL)

BUSINESS TRIP

Business trips are never a joy. They represent sterile rooms, skin-stripping soap and over-starched sheets – but it's not difficult to create a home from home. Our top tips on clothes are: first, take a variety of tops to make your business suit as versatile as possible; and second, take at least two spare pairs of perfect tights.

The main object here is to have a bag that you can easily swing into the overseat storage rack on a train, or to get on and off the airplane as fast as possible, which means hand luggage only.

CONTENTS

PHOTO OF LOVED ONE
Nice to wake up next to your man, even if he is two-dimensional.

SCENTED CANDLE
Pack one that you use at home to give your room a familiar aroma.

SHAMPOO AND CONDITIONER
Hotel freebies are usually shit.

EARPLUGS
You never know how thin hotel walls will be; also invaluable for cutting out background chitchat on train journeys and flights.

RADIO
Essential for Radio 4 listeners, who can pick up the Archers on LW or the World Service in a foreign country.

MUFTI
Comfy clothes to snuggle up in when business dinners are not the order of the night.

ALARM CLOCK
You can't afford to miss that meeting.

Muffles Wax
Earplugs
AVEDA
AVEDA
CAMOMILE
SHAMPOO

COUNTRY WEEKEND

It's true. Houses in the countryside are colder than those snug urban homes. The lack of community warmth generated from neighbouring houses slotted together in cosy streets is partly to blame. Out in the sticks Jack Frost, coupled with drafty corridors and antiquated central heating, gets an unfair opportunity to freeze one's bollocks to the bone.

Not that the bleak midwinter is the only time we take off on rural jaunts. Spring and summer, though warmer, have their own sets of hazards, like rain, mud and uneven terrain. Gloves and jeans should be clean, but not your very best – dogs produce an inordinate amount of saliva and hairs.

Country abodes will usually be kitted out with waterproofs and wellies, but the chances of finding an electric blanket or fluffy dressing gown are slim.

CONTENTS

SLIPPERS
Essential for corridor creeping on wooden or stone floors.

THERMAL UNDERWEAR
Good for damp, barely used beds and unheated dining rooms as well as wintery walks.

HAT
There will be raggedy ones on offer, so if you want grime-free headgear that looks good, bring your own.

WELLINGTON BOOTS
Again these will be on offer, but usually too large, too small or no longer waterproof.

COAT HANGERS
Never enough, and the meagre few are always wire.

ALARM CLOCK
Breakfast will often be between certain hours, so if you want hot coffee, rely on your clock and not a wake-up call.

HOT-WATER BOTTLE
For the aforementioned damp beds.

BATH OIL
A little luxury that is best bought in a small bottle or decanted into a plastic bottle.

HAIR DRYER
You could use the bar heater, but a dryer will be quicker.

RADIO
Nice to have a personal sound system.

PRESENT FOR HOSTESS
Take chocolates in case the food is shit, or send flowers before you arrive so that she can use them for the house party.

BRORA
PHILIPS

AIRPLANE

Long-haul flights are a killer whether you can afford posh class or not. The air stinks and dries out skin and eyes, the seats break your back. Your neighbour will keep his overhead light on all night, burrowed in some trashy novel he 'can't put down'. The erratic air conditioning will make you freeze one minute and hyperventilate the next. The only hyperactive toddler on the flight will be the other side of the bookworm and will find you more fascinating than the in-flight entertainment. Just as you are about to doze off, an officious brute of a stewardess will shake you from slumber with a plate of slop unfit for your worst enemy. Yes, flying is torture, but there are measures you can take to make it bearable.

CONTENTS

LARGE WOOL SCARF
To replace the revolting synthetic mesh blankets that make you sweat and itch.

BABY PILLOW OR NECK REST
To avoid whiplash and the need for an osteopath on landing.

PADDED EYE MASK
The plastic in-flight ones don't keep light out and ping off the back of your head every time you move a toenail.

WATER
Those mean plastic glasses go nowhere in rehydrating one's sapped body.

SWEAT PANTS
Don't get on the plane wearing these, but carry a pair to change into. They can be crumpled and spilt on and you won't care a toss.

TOOTHBRUSH AND PASTE
To combat the green cloud that emits from your mouth post-flight.

SLEEPING AID
Either in homeopathic or chemical form to make sleep a reality rather than a tortured yearning.

EYE DROPS
For sore red eyes.

VASELINE
For the areas that dry out first like nails and lips.

VAPORIZER
A freshener spray that instantly revives. This can be plain mineral water or a more exotic concoction of aromatherapy oils.

TOTAL CARE
ENERGISING
evian
Natural Mineral Water
PENGUIN CLASSICS
JANE AUSTEN
PERSUASION

SUMMER HOLIDAY

A summer holiday wardrobe is pretty basic in its content. Swimsuits, bikinis, sundresses, pretty shoes are all obvious. Luckily, clothes for a hot climate are light, which means we can take more. We can't stand those magazine articles that suggest you can wear a swimsuit with a skirt in the evening or advocate minimizing your wardrobe so it can fit into a sponge bag. Do you wait all year for a holiday to wear the same smeggy clothes day in, day out? No, no, no. You want to look lovely, fanciable and gorgeous. But don't forget that certain practical items are indispensable.

CONTENTS

SUNGLASSES

The most necessary summer item and the most easily left behind because you can never believe you would be stupid enough to do so.

SARONG

Obvious we know, but it can be used for so many different purposes: bed gear, screen to change behind on beach, towel.

SUNSCREEN FOR HAIR AND BODY

Don't count on buying this at your destination; you will only be able to find a local brand that you cannot rely on.

MOSQUITO REPELLENT

This and/or an antihistamine to combat those flying thugs.

BLOCKER UPPERS

Diarrhoea is always just around the corner.

SUN HAT

Best to get one you can fold into your case rather than have to carry on the plane like a prat.

PLASTIC SHOES

Saves burning feet on hot sand and stubbing toes in rocky waters.

RAZOR AND TWEEZERS

Hair grows faster in hot weather.

BOOKS

Not for relaxation, but the kind that will inform you on what to do where you are.

ADAPTER PLUGS

For hair dryer, personal stereo, etc.

BATTERIES

For those times when your personal stereo runs out of juice on that secluded beach.

Imodium
Can stop diarrhoea with one dose
12 ANTI-DIARRHOEAL CAPSULES
AUTAN
ACTIVE
AVEDA
AVEDA
INSIGHT GUIDES
ISTANBUL
DURACELL
DURACELL
NORTHERN EUROPE

WINTER SKIING

Like the summer holiday kit, your winter gear won't change a whole lot, but because keeping warm means bulky clothes, these will take up a lot of space. When packing ski socks, however many you think you'll need, add an extra pair to be worn while the others are drying. Ski suit, boots etc are big and clumsy, so you need to be economical with stuff you sport après-ski. You will have to cut down on things like trousers, tops, disco skirts but the following items will make or break your holiday if you take or leave them behind.

CONTENTS

WARM HAT
60% of body heat escapes from your head, so the warmer your bonnet, the snugger your body.
GLOVE LINERS AND SHOE LINERS
Fingers are the first to suffer from frostbite, while cold toes make for misery and bad ski style.
HAND WARMERS
Fantastic when your gloves give in to the wet and the cold.
RUBBER SOLED BOOTS
To prevent you going ass over tit walking down the street to a restaurant, but take nice ones that don't look ridiculous indoors.
SUNGLASSES
Remember you can only wear goggles on the slope.
HIP FLASK
For a little nip to keep you warm and give Dutch courage.
PASSPORT PHOTO
So you don't have to queue up for your ski pass.
SUN BLOCK
Just because it's cold doesn't mean the sun doesn't burn.
TRAVEL WASH
Saves on hotel cleaning prices and keeps knickers and socks smelling sweet.
WALKMAN
For when you're waiting for friends to return from the slopes.
CHOCOLATE
Emergency rations.

TRAVEL
CLEAN
HEAT factory
For Continuous Warmth Anytime... Anywhere
SONY
MD
Milka

WORLD TOUR

Where the fuck to begin? Not in your wardrobe, that's for sure, unless you are rich enough to have hundreds of lackeys lugging your suitcases from continent to continent. For us of mortal means it's a much better idea to buy clothing as you go, thus leaving room in your backpack for emergency bits and pieces.

CONTENTS

FIRST AID KIT
Intravenous needles etc are a must when travelling to many foreign parts, where sterile kit is not always an option.

CREDIT CARD
Be sure your card is accepted around the world. Less nickable than cash and can be cancelled and re-issued if necessary.

SUNGLASSES
An expensive pair will keep up appearances, while a cheap pair could provide you with an emergency bargaining tool.

BOOTS
Good, sturdy, comfortable walking boots are worth investing in. The more you pay the better they'll be and the longer they'll last. Breaking them in before departure is advisable.

INSECT REPELLENT
Where the hell are you going to get this when you need it halfway down the Amazon?

SUNSCREEN
You can buy it abroad, but for the same reason that you need to take repellent, keep a secret supply of good sun block.

FOLDING SUN HAT
You can buy these as you go, but we find there is something rather romantic about a hat that travels the world.

BOOKS
Travel books relevant to the places you visit make them come alive. Novels, because the English books found in hotels are usually Mills & Boon or other crap with missing pages.

MOBILE PHONE
Phone cards, reverse charges, credit card calls are all possibilities, but you can't beat a mobile for instant accessibility to the rest of the world.

TORCH
For power cuts and unlit streets.

GREENLAND
(Grønland)
Essential for European Motoring
Suitable for Car or Home
Contents:
AID KIT
UK CLNET
GF768
VISA
EGYPT
SUDAN
CENTRAL AFRICAN REPUBLIC
CAMEROON
DEM. REP. OF CONGO
ANGOLA
LANCÔME
SÔLEIL
ULTRA
50
PEAUX SENSIBLES AU SOLEIL
SUN SENSITIVE SKINS
AUTAN
ACTIVE
INSECT REPELLENT
PUMP SPRAY
GARNIER
AMBRE SOLAIRE
AFTER SUN
TAN MAINTAINER
FOR A LONGER LASTING TAN
FACE AND BODY
Collins
SINGA
INDIAN OCEAN
SOUTH
OCEAN
THE WORLD

SUMMARY

In this chapter we have not given a step by step guide to what you should take, because we don't know what your wardrobe holds. What we do know are the essentials and little extras that one would be lost without, were they left behind. Prescription packing becomes a doddle when you have done It once, and when you have the contents sorted, all that's left is how to put it in the actual suitcase.

Contrary to typical methods, place your most crease-prone pieces at the bottom, working up to shoes, cosmetics, appliances and books. No bumpy bulk at the bottom means your clothes will lie flatter and the weight of the heavier goods will give them a good pressing en route. Have a safe trip!

THE TEN COMMANDMENTS

1. At the end of each holiday, make a list of what you actually wear – and don't pack any more on your next holiday.
2. If there is something you can't live without, take it with you in case you can't get it where you are going.
3. Always make sure you have enough money on your credit card before your holiday.
4. Always take out separate travel insurance.
5. Put hidden name tags on your luggage.
6. Don't put valuables in the hold – keep them in your hand luggage.
7. If you are staying in a hotel, put valuables in the safe in your room or with the concierge.
8. If you are going to a country with strong religious customs, find out and respect their dress code.
9. Cosmetics are nearly always more expensive abroad – but cheaper at the airport.
10. In hot climates, you will be able to buy a sunhat abroad – it will be cheaper and take up no room in your suitcase.

DIRECTORY

HAIR

BIRMINGHAM

Stuart Crown
City Plaza
First Floor
47 Crown Street
Birmingham B2 5EF
Tel: 0121 633 0440
⌚ Mon–Fri 9–6, Thur 9–7,
Sat 9–5.30
American Express/Diners Club not accepted
This salon is laid back and relaxed, styling is fashionably spot on. The salon is very good on cutting, colours and real hair extensions. It has good disabled access from the Plaza lifts and cutting chairs can be moved to accommodate wheelchairs.

Umberto Giannini
The Waters Edge
Brindley Place
Broad Street
Birmingham B1 2HL
Tel: 0121 633 0111
Fax: 0121 633 2888
e-mail: einfo@umbertogiannini.co.uk
web-site: www.umbertogiannini.co.uk
⌚ Mon, Tue, Wed 10–7, Thur & Fri 10–8, Sat 8.30–5
American Express/Diners Club not accepted
Manager and colourist Lisa Shepherd (1998 Midlands Hairdresser of the Year) heads a talented staff that at the time of writing had been nominated in two categories of the 1999 British Hairdressing Awards. Umberto himself is available on average once a week, when he's not doing BBC *Style Challenge* and other high-profile TV. The atmosphere is mellow and jazzy and the salon is disabled-friendly. Additional branches: Seven more salons in the West Midlands. Phone 01384 444771 for details.

James Kimber
138 New Street
Birmingham B2 4NS
Tel: 0121 643 6111
⌚ Mon, Tue, Wed & Sat 9–6, Thur & Fri 9–7
American Express/Diners Club not accepted
This friendly salon has a strong following of clients. Quality standards are maintained by a team of top stylists who are all trained in house. Although up-market, pretentious is something that the salon is not. It caters for all ages and tastes and boasts an extensive variety of services, from extensions to Afro-Caribbean styles. The manager believes that consultation is very important and welcomes any potential client to discuss any hair service. Refreshments are provided and food supplied at a cost.

BRISTOL

Jay Jays
7 Clouds Hill Road
St George
Bristol BS5 7LD
Tel: 0117 955 7751
Fax: 0117 904 9989
⌚ Mon 9–4, Wed 8.30–5, Tue & Thur 8.30–7, Fri & Sat 8.30–5.30
As well as high-quality cuts and colouring, Jay Jays specializes in long-hair work and colour correction. Stylists are also specially trained to deal discreetly with hair loss problems. The salon works a lot with natural products and herbal colours and provides therapeutic massages and aromatherapy. Some stylists will do combined hair and make-up. Sandwiches can be arranged if clients phone in the order in the morning. Wheelchair access is available at the Sandwell Road salon.
Additional branches: Sandwell Road, Bristol.

Toni & Guy
1–2 Augustine's Parade
Bristol BS1 4XJ
Tel: 0117 930 0077
e-mail: salon@bristol.toniandguy.co.uk
web-site: www.toniandguy.co.uk
⌚ Mon 10–5.30, Tue 9.15–4,
Wed 11–6.30, Thur 10–7,
Fri 10–5.30, Sat 9–4.30
American Express/Diners Club not accepted
This salon is a comparatively new and very well received addition to Bristol. Covering all cutting and technical services, the salon is everything you might expect from the best of Toni & Guy. When a cut and technical service is combined both stylists will speak to the client together to ensure that the best total look is achieved. No dry cuts.

DUBLIN

Cowboys & Angels
4 St William Street
Dublin 2
Tel: (00 353) 1 679 7654
⌚ Mon, Tue, Fri 10–6.30, Wed, Thur 9.30–5, Sat 9.30–5
American Express/Diners Club/Switch not accepted
Best known for their very unusual dyes, Cowboys & Angels are also the people to go to for extensions. All ages are made welcome. Friendly and lively, the salon boasts a loyal following who come back again and again; it holds information cards on clients' past styles and colours. Free consultations to clients wishing to discuss options and receive recommendations from their stylist. Refreshments and sandwiches are offered. Easy access for disabled.

Lunatic Fringe
69 Grafton Street
Dublin 2
Tel: (00 353) 1 679 3766
⌚ Mon–Fri 9.30–6, Thur 9.30–8.30, Sat 9–6
This very up-beat salon verges on the mad. The company does not believe in overcharging and everything from extensions to classic cuts are available at great prices. The décor is colourful, the atmosphere very relaxed, and funky music is always on offer. There are bean-bags in the window where you and your friends can hang out with a coffee while waiting. The salon also features a nail boutique. Children welcome. No wheelchair access.

The Natural Cut
34 Wicklow Street
Dublin 2
Tel: (00 353) 1 679 7130
⌚ Mon–Sat 10–7
Cash and cheques only
Shane Boyd, owner and founder, specializes in dry cuts and believes a hairstyle should be achieved through the cut, without products or blow-drying. This is very refreshing news for those of us who try to re-create a salon style and end up looking like an amateur let loose with a far-too-powerful hairdryer. A one-hour appointment consists of a chat between the client and stylist, working together to create something suitable. As the hair is cut dry, no more agonizing neckache from poorly designed wash basins. Just a spritz with a spray and the cut. Shane has started providing colour services, but only subtle, natural colours 'which add a dimension to the cut.' The salon has a music-free but friendly, relaxed atmosphere to encourage chat between the client and stylist in the softly lit 'boudoir' setting.

GLASGOW

The Rainbow Room

30 George Square
Glasgow G2 1EG
Tel: 0141 226 3451
⏲ Mon–Fri 7.30–7.30, Thur 7.30–8.30, Sat 9–5, Sun 11.30–5.30
Linda Stewart prides her salons on the absence of specific technical departments: all her stylists are fully trained in every area of hair services, cutting and colouring. They perform an abundance of colour work. Every client has a complementary Shiatsu head massage; while this is quite common these days, this salon has offered this service for 14 years – they were obviously one of the original head massage trendsetters. Music is chosen to reflect the mood of the salon, for example on a Monday morning the music reflects a calm, relaxing mood, while on a Friday the sounds will be jazzy, upbeat salsa, to inspire the client for the weekend ahead. The 3,500 ft George Square salon is a Design Award winner. The small, attached shop sells a wide range of products, including the salon's own line. The owner's philosophy is that the salons, working in conjunction with each other, have also become their own competition, and rightly maintain the company's high standards.
Additional branches: Buchanan Street, Glasgow. Tel: 0141 248 5300
24 Royal Exchange Square, Glasgow. Tel: 0141 204 4460

Rita Rusk International

498 Great Western Road
Glasgow G12 8EW
Tel: 0141 357 3333
⏲ Mon, Tue, Wed & Fri 9–6, Thur 9–8, Sat 9–5
American Express/Diners Club not accepted
Rita Rusk prides itself on its uniformity of excellence. All of the stylists and technicians are in-house trained and the only way to a future in the company is through the system. The company has a multi-national artistic team and does not promote any specific products. The only items on sale are professional scissors. One level of the Great Western Road salon has facilities for the disabled. There is also a beauty franchise within that salon.
Additional branches: Westnile Street, Glasgow. Tel: 0141 221 1472

Taylor Ferguson

106 Bath Street
Glasgow G2 2EN
Tel: 0141 331 1728
⏲ Mon–Wed 9–6, Thur 8.45–7.30, Fri 9–6.30, Sat 9–5
American Express/Diners Club/Switch not accepted
A blend of serious styling and very relaxed personal service is the key to Taylor Ferguson's success. Cutting standards are tight but the friendly staff ensure that the mood is laid back. The salon is large enough to provide private room facilities, making it the popular choice for clients with medical problems and celebrities. Backwash basins are suitable for disabled clients. With a restaurant downstairs and a beauty salon attached, why not make a day of it?

LEEDS

Aveda Concept Salon

Harvey Nichols
Fourth Floor
107 Briggate
Leeds LS1 6AZ
Tel: 0113 244 0212
Fax: 0113 244 1341
⏲ Mon, Tue & Wed 10–6, Thur & Fri 10–7, Sat 9–7
The Aveda Concept has spread with Harvey Nichols to Leeds. And what exactly is that concept? Environmentally friendly natural products and colours, the relaxed energy of a *feng shui* beechwood salon, and technical and cutting expertise. Every cut is accompanied by a complementary scalp and shoulder stress-relief massage and a post-cut make-up touch-up. The salon is wheelchair accessible. Lunches can be ordered from the Harvey Nichols restaurant.

LONDON

Roger Britnell at Richard Ward

162b Sloane Street
London SW1 9BS
Tel: 020 7245 6151
⏲ Mon–Sat 9–6
Gives the best haircut in London. We both trusted him enough to chop off our locks. He is an artist and a genius.

John Frieda

4 Aldford Street
London W1Y 5PU
Tel: 020 7499 3617
⏲ Mon–Sat 9–5 (earlier and later by arrangement)
American Express/Diners Club not accepted
The name John Frieda is synonymous with a world-leading creative team and a high-profile (deservedly so) product range. His London salons live up to the reputation of their founder and remain the places to go for some of the best cuts in town.
Additional branches: 75 New Cavendish Street, London W1M 7RB. Tel: 020 7636 1401

Daniel Galvin

42–44 George Street
London W1H 5RE
Tel: 020 7486 8601
Fax: 020 7487 2616
e-mail: hair@daniel-galvin.co.uk
web-site: www.daniel-galvin.co.uk
⏲ Mon–Sat 8.30–6.30
Diners Club not accepted
Daniel Galvin is known as 'the King of colour'. The first to specialize in hair colour back in the 1970s, today his salon is renowned the world over as the centre of colour excellence. The high standards of his salon team ensure that you'll walk away from the friendly, comfortable modern-classic salon with a beautiful natural finish. The salon is wheelchair friendly. An in-house menu is available.

Daniel Hersheson

45 Conduit Street
London W1R 9FB
Tel: 020 7434 1747
Fax: 020 7437 5540
⏲ Mon–Sat 9–6
Diners Club not accepted
Daniel Hersheson is a high-profile Mayfair salon with a reputation for creativity and innovation. The salon includes a separate technical department and boasts over 20 stylists, all of whom have been trained by Daniel. Daniel's son Luke has his own high-profile reputation and has done fashion work for the *Observer*, *Sunday Times Style*, *Tank* and *Marie Claire*. The modern, three-floor salon is simple and stylish, and the philosophy throughout is about distinction, progress and individuality. Breakfast, lunch and tea are available. The salon's hot waxing and nail services are also excellent. Arrangements can be made for disabled customers.

Charles Worthington

7 Percy Street
London W1P 9FB
Tel: 020 7631 1370
⏲ Mon–Sat 10–6
This is the newest in the Charles Worthington line. As expected, standards are high and Charles is available there himself on average twice a week. However you'll need to book him early to beat his two-month waiting list. Stylist Jo Rapley, Newcomer of The Year 1998, works from this salon. A lunch menu is available. The Triton Square salon is the most disabled-friendly, Tel: 020 7383 4840.
Additional branches: Four other London salons. Phone 020 7631 1370 for details.

MANCHESTER

Andrew Collinge

11 Chapel Walks
Manchester M2 1HN
Tel: 0161 834 1616
Fax: 0161 834 1767
web-site: www.andrewcollinge.com
⏲ Mon,Tue, Wed 10–7, Thur & Fri 10–7.45, Sat 8.30–5.30
At Andrew Collinge standards are high across the board, since all stylists benefit from training at one of the biggest and best hairdressing academies in the country. The modern-classic décor has an elegant feel and the mood of the neutral copper and cream tones is very relaxed. Extra

touches include a salon menu – starting from sandwiches at £3.95 – and a Make-Up-To-Go service. This five-minute post-styling treat, from technicians expertly trained by Liz Collinge, is good for reviving post-colour fatigue.

Nicky Oliver
32 Oldham Street
Manchester M1 1JN
Tel: 0161 236 0644
Fax: 0161 236 2407
⌚ Mon, Tue & Wed 9–6, Thur 10–7, Fri, Sat 9–6
Inside this very distinctive salon, designed by Philippe Starck, you'll find specialists in both cutting and colour. Staff are all trained in the company school – and customer care is as important as technical skill. Disabled access is good since the salon is spacious and entry is possible via a lift.

NEWCASTLE

Barry and Bobby Hair Design
50 St Andrew's Road
Newcastle NE1 5SF
Tel: 0191 232 5791 / 232 2354
Fax: 0191 232 0101
⌚ Mon 9–5, Tue–Fri 9–6, Sat 9–5
This neo-classical black-and-white salon spread across two floors has a team of 22, who provide welcoming, high-quality hairdressing services for all ages. The salon specializes in colouring, Afro-Caribbean and bridal work. The ground floor of the salon is wheelchair accessible but technical treatments (usually done in the basement) can all be brought upstairs. A full range of beauty treatments is also available in the salon, including skin care, manicures, pedicures, waxing and vertical tanning. The salon has its own great range of products, The Barry and Bobby Hair Design Collection, as well as carrying a massive retail range. Children and dogs are welcome.

Boilerhouse
7 Acorn Road
Jesmond
Newcastle NE2 2DJ
Tel: 0191 281 2348
⌚ Mon–Fri 9–5, Thur 9–7, Sat 8.30–4
Cash and cheques only
Owners Steve and Kim, both ex-Vidal Sassoon, ensure that all staff are in-house trained and work their way up as stylists who offer a high standard of excellence across the board. However, Boilerhouse prides itself on its cutting skills. No tongs or round brushes are used, and the salon refuses to set hair. Everything is in the cut, and a hands-on touch is used to create a very natural finish. As they say themselves, 'we don't cut corners'. Children are welcome. Sandwiches can be sent out for.

Gary Hooker Hairdressing
Swallows Gosforth Park Hotel
High Gosforth Park
Newcastle NE3 5HN
Tel: 0191 217 0217
⌚ Mon, Tue & Wed 9.30–5, Thur 9.30–6.30, Fri 10.30–8, Sat 9–5
At Gary Hooker a very flexible approach is taken; the aim is to create a 'just ask and you can have it' experience. The salon prides itself on the award-winning ability of key members of staff. Gary Hooker has been Northern Hairdresser of the Year three times. His partner Michael Young has won the same prize, as well as being awarded the L'Oreal Colour Trophy three times. A wide range of foods, wines and treats is available. A beauty salon is adjacent, so many people make a day of it. Disabled access to the salon is easy via a permanent ramp and lift.

MOPS Hairdressing
Ground Floor
1–2 Gallowgate
Newcastle NE1 4SG
Tel: 0191 232 9559
Fax: 0191 261 5561
⌚ Mon & Tue 9–6, Wed 9–5.15, Thur 9.45–8.15, Fri 10–7.30, Sat 8.45–6
This well-established salon often works in conjunction with Wella. The in-house trained styling team will take time to find the right style for you, whether it be a modern head-turner or a classic cut with a twist. The salon is very strong on consultation and will advise you on the cut to suit not only your face shape but your lifestyle…or maybe just a touch of colour to create a whole new look. The salon is light and airy and because of its size has good wheelchair access.

BEAUTY

BIRMINGHAM

Umberto Giannini Beauty
The Waters Edge
Brindley Place
Broad Street
Birmingham B1 2HL
Tel: 0121 633 0111
Fax: 0121 633 2888
e-mail: einfo@umbertogiannini.co.uk
web-site: www.umbertogiannini.co.uk
⌚ Mon,Tue, Wed 10–7, Thur & Fri 10–8, Sat 8.30–5
American Express/Diners Club not accepted
As part of a total day out you might want to pop upstairs from the Umberto Giannini hair salon (see Hairdressers) for a treatment with Vicky at Umberto Giannini Beauty. Choose from a variety of treatments including facials, a 40-minute Swedish massage, or a full body aromatherapy session. Other excellent but less tempting necessities include various waxing services.

BRISTOL

The Temple (formerly Origin)
The Swallow Royal Hotel
College Green
Bristol BS1 5TA
Tel: 0117 927 3389
⌚ Mon–Wed 10–6, Thur & Fri 10–7, Sat & Sun 10–6
American Express/Diners Club not accepted
The Temple is about purity and luxury. Treatments are holistic and the applications are hands-on, not technological. The calm sanctuary atmosphere, situated alongside ancient Roman baths, is a perfect complement to the harmonizing aromatherapy and reflexology treatments. A Full Sanctuary Day (£150) includes 2 hours of beauty and hair treatments, over 3 hours of swimming pool, spa, steamroom, and air-conditioned gym access, and a healthy two-course lunch with wine. Facials £18–£50, full body massage £40. Manicures, pedicures and waxing treatments come particularly well recommended. Gift vouchers are available.

DUBLIN

The Beauty Room
19 Drury Street
Dublin 2
Tel: (00 353) 1 677 4093
⌚ Mon–Wed 9–7, Thur 9–8.30, Fri 9–7.30, Sat 9–6
Cash and cheques only
This quaint little salon is known for a perfect job with that special personal touch. Known by word of mouth, clients just keep on recommending it and popping back for more. Treatments include facials (£25), waxing, eyelash tinting and a great back massage (£10).

Frances Bergin Nails
Tel: (00 353) 0 872657702
⌚ Mon–Fri 10–8 (by appointment only)
Cash and cheques only
Mobile nail technician Frances brings very sociable treatment to clients in the comfort of their own homes. This convenient style is so popular that whenever she mentions moving to a static salon her clients complain. All manicures and pedicures include a basic massage (from £35).

Bliss
30 Sandycove Road
Sandycove
County Dublin
Tel: (00 353) 1 280 8345
⌚ Mon, Tue & Fri 9.30–6, Wed,Thur 9.30–8, Sat 10–5, Sun 11–6
Owner Claire McKeon comes direct from the consumer side of the business. Being a journalist, she knows exactly what clients want and has her finger on the pulse of the constantly changing beauty world. The salon received its first review from *Image* magazine, notoriously hard to impress, who voted Bliss the 'hottest' salon in Dublin, and it's easy to see why. Claire believes all clients should be treated like royalty. Clients visit this salon to be truly pampered in an impressively soothing atmosphere. There are four massage rooms, sound-proofed to aid relaxation, and a great team, who offer a range of nine body and four head massages. Facials from £20–£40, Indian head massage £18, back massage £23, Shiatsu full body

massage £28. The salon sells a range of top brand products, as well as an unusual range of totally natural soaps with names like 'Irish Bog Peat' and 'Spring H20', hand-made in the country by two hippies.

Buttercups Face and Body Clinic
26a Powers Court Town House
Dublin 2
Tel: (00 353) 1 679 4866
⏲ Mon–Wed 9–7, Thur 9–8.30, Fri 9–7.30, Sat 9–6
American Express/Diners Club/Switch not accepted
Company philosophy revolves around putting clients at ease. The staff 'specialize in everything' and the list of usual and more unusual treatments is almost endless. Treatments include aromatherapy, reflexology, and a great range of facials (from £35). Depending on your choice a visit to the salon might leave you toned, detoxified or stress-relieved. Clients can make appointments weeks in advance, yet can also walk in straight off the street due to the sheer size of the salon.
Additional branches: Johnson Place, Dublin. Tel: (00 353) 1 845 0787 ⏲ Open late most nights.
The Grand Hotel, Malahide. Tel: (00 353) 1 845 0787 ⏲ Open Sundays.
The Hill, Stillorgan. Tel: (00 353) 1 283 1459 ⏲ Open late most nights.

GLASGOW

Leah-Brooklyn Beauty and Nails
143 Cumbernauld Road
Stepps
Glasgow G33 6EY
Tel: 0141 779 4949/ 0141 779 9902
⏲ Tues, Wed 10–6, Thur, Fri 10–8, Sat 10–5, Sun 12–5 (by appointment). Closed Mon.
Cash and cheques only
Moya Wren, an educator for the Creative Nails Academy in Glasgow, really knows her stuff when it comes to nails. Her salon is professional, friendly and inviting, and uses only Creative Nails products. If your own nails are strong and shapely, you might like a SPA manicure (£15) or pedicure. Using the Creative Nails nail enhancements system (from £35) you can choose from a permanent French manicure, which can then be left natural or painted, or seamless under-nail extensions. A diagnostic process is used to create the right shape to suit your hands and lifestyle. There is also a semi-permanent make-up specialist.

The Rainbow Room
30 George Square
Glasgow G2 1EG
Tel: 0141 226 3451
⏲ Mon–Fri 7.30–7.30, Thur 7.30–8.30, Sat 9–5, Sun 11.30–5.30
The Rainbow Room (see Hairdressers) has an in-house beauty section with five treatment rooms, offering a very wide choice of treatments: massage, facials, waxing, electrolysis, manicures, pedicures, reflexology, flotation room, sauna, algae and mud wraps.
Additional branches: See Hairdressers, Glasgow.

LEEDS

Designer Nails
247 Otley Road
West Park
Leeds LS16 5LQ
Tel: 0113 230 4305
⏲ Phone for details
American Express/Diners Club not accepted
This salon's team of eight technicians offer a range of liquid and powder nails using high-quality Creative Nails products. The salon is fully ventilated so you won't be coming out high as a kite. Profile records are maintained for clients. There is also an in-house beautician for waxing and facials.

LEEDS (YORK)

Absolute Bodycare
12 Blake Street
York YL1 8QG
Tel: 01904 625500
⏲ Mon–Wed 9–6, Thur–Fri 9–7, Sat 9–5
American Express/Diners Club not accepted
This friendly salon has a reputation for being the first in the area to get its hands on brand new treatments. The mood is always relaxing, but it is wise to book ahead for the busy end-of-week appointment times. Treatments include facials (£17.50–£33), massages (back, £17.50, body £27.50) and a very popular eyelash perming service (£30.95).

LONDON

Bharti Vyas Holistic Therapy and Beauty Centre
5 & 24 Chiltern Street
London W1M 1HB
Tel: (appointments) 020 7935 5312; (information) 020 7486 7167
Fax: 020 7224 3382
e-mail: bhartivyas.co.uk
web-site: www.bharti-vyas.co.uk
⏲ Mon–Sat 9.30–6
Bharti Vyas has been a holistic therapist for over 20 years and her clients include many well-known faces. The salons are run on her philosophy that beauty on the outside begins on the inside. Treatments include facials, body treatments, magnet therapy, skin tag and laser hair removal.

Charlotte Storey at Daniel Hersheson
45 Conduit Street
London W1R 9FB
Tel: 020 7434 1747
Fax: 020 7437 5540
⏲ Tue–Sat 9–6 (can be flexible outside these hours)
Highly recommended Charlotte Storey is part of a small team of manicurists who provide manicures (from £20) and pedicures (from £30) either as an independent service or in combination with hair treatments at this salon.

Eve Lom Complexions
2 Spanish Place
London W1M 5AN
Tel: 020 7935 9988
Fax: 020 7224 0515
e-mail: evelom.co.uk
⏲ Tue–Sat 9–5
Cash and cheques only
The key words with Eve Lom are pure, natural, gentle and simple. Eve uses no steam, mechanical or electrically stimulated techniques. To quote Eve: 'I want to get the skin working again by itself, by exfoliating and restoring the natural tone. If I have a message, it is 'exfoliate, exfoliate, exfoliate!' Eve's trademark is her craniosacral work, a natural beauty therapy that works on what is under the skin: muscle, nerves and tendons. Eve Lom Facial (1 1/2 hours) £140 with Eve Lom and £100 with a senior therapist. Eve Lom Ultimate Cleanse (1 hour) £65.
Mail-order: Tel: 020 8661 7991

The French Cosmetic Medical Company
25 Wimpole Street
London W1M 7AD
Tel: 020 7637 0548
Fax: 020 7637 5110
e-mail: doctor@frenchcosmetic.com
⏲ Mon–Fri 9–6, Sat 9–12
This company is constantly at the forefront of cosmetic development. Dr Sebag is highly recommended for his line and buttock treatments (line treatments from £400, buttocks fom £200), and his laser resurfacing. His extreme accuracy has made him the choice of the stars around the world. Cécile is a qualified beautician and medical nurse; her treatments, known as 'cosmetical', cross the line between pharmaceutical and cosmetic. She specializes in peeling (from £80) and revitalization treatments. Dr Sister specializes in made-to-measure diets, using natural but powerful plant formulas (one-month diet from £80).

Lynette Macintosh at The Nail Bar
37 Maddox Street
London W1R 9LD
Tel: 020 7499 5898
⏲ Mon–Fri 10–7, Sat 11–6
Creative Master Lynette Macintosh comes hotly recommended. She prides herself on giving the perfect pedicure, which is a treat for the entire foot, not just the nails. The nail bar is, as it sounds, a New York-style salon, where you are treated at the zigzag bar with drink in hand (non-alcoholic of course). The atmosphere is fun and unintimidating but nail matters are taken very seriously. Manicures (from £15) and pedicures (from £20) come in French, deluxe, or re-shape and re-varnish varieties. Nail extensions can be acrylic, fibreglass or gel. Waxing and eyelash/brow tinting are also available.

MANCHESTER

The Beauty Box
77a Park Lane
Poynton
Cheshire SK12 1RD
Tel: 01625 871115
⌚ Mon & Fri 9.30–5.30, Tue & Thur 9–7.30. Closed Wed & alternate Sat
Cash and cheques only
The Beauty Box, though small, is wonderfully bright and provides a welcome contrast to the larger salons that some find intimidating and impersonal. Services include electrolysis, waxing, facials (from £10) and manicures/pedicures (from £6.50/£7.20).

Malmaison
Piccadilly
Manchester M1 3AQ
Tel: 0161 278 1000
⌚ Mon–Sun (phone for details)
Le Petit Spa at Malmaison offers a range of treatments and tonics designed to help you physically and mentally relax, pamper and tone. Treatments range from the 30-minute Express Facial (£20) to full-day holistic and restorative treats. For a day of relaxation try the E'SPA Holistic (£75); or for the height of decadence, Indulgence (£95) is a full day of total harmonizing and pampering. If something a bit more active is to your taste, try Revitalize and Energize (£75), a half-day that begins with a fitness assessment. The salon uses exclusively E'SPA products, a collection of deeply relaxing aromatherapy oils, revitalizing seaweeds and nourishing skin care. Who couldn't benefit from the Luxury Face and Bust Treatment (£45)? The salon also has specially devised Pre- and Post-natal treatments (£45).

NEWCASTLE

Dream Day Spa (formerly French Beauty)
20 Great North Road
Jesmond
Newcastle NE2 4PS
Tel: 0191 230 2269
⌚ Mon–Sun 9–7 (by appointment)
American Express/Diners Club not accepted
Expanded and in a brand new location this is more an urban spa than a traditional salon. Sally French heads a small team, who specialize in really personalized treatment. The salon offers various facials (non surgical face lift, £35; 2 hour Total Youth Beauty Treatment including anti-ageing facial £60), eyelash perming, waxing, slimming wraps, manicure/pedicures (from £8), including sculptured nails and nail art treatments, vertical tanning and body bronzing (body treatments from £25).

Malmaison
Quayside
Newcastle NE1 3DX
Tel: 0191 245 5000
⌚ Mon–Sun (phone for details)
Range of treatments as at Malmaison in Manchester.

SPECIALIST DRY-CLEANERS

BIRMINGHAM

John Buckley Cleaner of Fine Clothes
1a Old Warwick Road
Hockley Heath
Solihull B94 6HH
Tel: 01564 782 953
Fax: 01564 785 110
⌚ Mon–Fri 8–5.30, Sat 9–1
American Express/Diners Club not accepted
Over 30 years in the business has established John Buckley's reputation. The three branches are recommended by most retailers within a 20–mile radius. Alteration services are available.
Additional branches: Stratford upon Avon. Tel: 01789 297819
Solihull. Tel: 01564 777561

Elegance
183 Church Road
Yardly
Birmingham B25 8UR
Tel: 0121 784 6107
⌚ Mon–Sat 9–5
Cash and cheques only
A specialist cleaner that won't put your favourite garments at risk.
Additional branches: Streetly, Sutton Coldfield. Tel: 0121 353 8420
Aldridge. Tel: 01922 745144

DUBLIN

Craft Cleaners
12 Upper Baggot Street
Dublin 4
Tel: (00 353) 1 668 8198
⌚ Mon–Fri 7.30–7, Sat 8.30–6
No credit cards
The owners of this specialist dry-cleaners think of themselves as actors, always judged on their last performance. The fact that they have been going strong for 28 years without advertising is the best proof of the quality of that performance. Craft Cleaners specialize in a hand finish and will sew on any loose buttons at the same time. They also have a New York branch.

LYKNU
4 The Mall
Donnybrooke
Dublin 4
Tel (00 353) 1 269 2609
Fax: (00 353) 1 269 4302
⌚ Mon–Sat 7.45–6
American Express/Diners Club/Laser/Switch not accepted
LYKNU (pronounced Like New) are dry-cleaning, preservation and restoration specialists. Often working for museums and antique clothing retailers, these are the people to trust with heirlooms and intricate garments. They also deal with standard dry-cleaning and basic alterations.

GLASGOW

Clark Thomas (Tailors)
(See alterations)

LEEDS

Classic Cleaners
Unit 3
63 Town Street
Leeds LS12 1XD
Tel: 0113 279 6237
⌚ Mon–Sat 8.30–5
Cash and cheques only
This highly recommended specialist cleaners gives all garments a quality hand finish. The company combines the latest technology with an environmental approach. Regular customers include Jigsaw and Harvey Nichols.

LONDON

Lewis & Wayne
13–15 Elystan Street
London SW3
Tel: 020 7589 5730
Fax: 020 7589 5075
⌚ Mon–Fri 8.30–1, 2–5.30,
Sat 8.30–12.30 Cash and cheques only
Lewis & Wayne clean discreetly for the country's most discerning individuals and the top fashion houses. Every garment is treated as the individual it is. Labels, buttons and trimmings are studied, and removed if necessary before treatment. Stain removal is handled by one individual with over 25 years experience and hand pressing is shared by a skilled team.

Additional branches: 7 Elystan Street (hand laundry service available).

Peters & Falla
281 New King's Road
London SW6
Tel: 020 7731 3255
⏲ Mon–Sat 8.30–6, Thur 8.30–2, Sat 9.30–5
Cash and cheques only
All garments are personally cleaned by Mr Falla; if you have any dry-cleaning queries you can speak to him direct on 020 7720 4490. The company is also rare in that it has a machine, available at very few specialist cleaners, that uses particularly gentle chemicals – especially good for beaded delicates and cashmere. Recommended by Armani and Harrod's leather and suede department. Delivery is possible in the West End and south London.
Additional branches: 179 New King's Road. Tel: 020 7731 5114

Upstage Theatrical Dry Cleaners
Unit 7–8 Acorn Production Centre
105 Blundell Street
London N7
Tel: 020 7609 9119
⏲ Mon–Fri 7–5
Cash and cheques only
The choice of the West End and numerous national theatre companies, Upstage regularly deals with garments worth thousands of pounds, so can be confidently trusted with your designer outfits and family heirlooms. Due to the nature of the majority of its trade, Upstage is the place to turn in an emergency for morning to afternoon service. Garments can be collected by TNT, and delivered back to your door (to fit in with the West End runs).
Mail-order: Garments can be posted or collected by TNT.

MANCHESTER

Granada Dry Cleaners
71–73 Bridge Street
Manchester M3 2RH
Tel: 0161 834 8947
Fax: 0161 832 0081
⏲ Mon–Fri 8–6, Sat 9–1
American Express/Diners Club not accepted
The company believes in an old-fashioned approach and embraces new technology only when it is the best tool for the job. Although all staff are highly trained in the art of cleaning you can be assured that any difficult decisions will be handled by the owner Ronny Singer. Granada also offers an in-house alterations service.
Additional branches: Prestwich, Manchester. Tel: 0161 798 5550

NEWCASTLE

Barringtons Valet Service
40 Cedar Road
Fenham
Newcastle NE4 9XX
Tel: 0191 274 1272
Fax: 0191 245 4646
⏲ Mon–Fri 9–5.30, Sat 9–2
Barringtons comes highly recommended, both in the area and nationally. A larger operation than many of the specialist cleaners recommended in this book, but in this case size does not mean that corners will be cut. The company will ably deal with delicate, leather and suede garments as well as laundry. In terms of alterations Barringtons offers services from replacing a lost button through to major re-styling work.
Mail-order: Post garments with instructions
Additional branches: Old Street, Newcastle city centre.
Phone 0191 274 1272 for a brochure including other agents.

DYERS

LONDON

Chalfont Dyers
222 Baker Street
London NW1 5RT
Tel: 0207 935 7316
⏲ Mon–Fri 8.30–6, Sat 9–1
Established more than 50 years, Chalfont Dyers deals only with natural fabrics, and will always talk the client through the risks of the dyeing process. Allow 3–6 weeks to dye a garment. Price on consultation; payment 75% in advance.

ALTERATIONS

BIRMINGHAM

The Ditty Box
1 Chester Road
Stonnall
Near Walsall
West Midlands WS9 9HH
Tel: 01922 459709/07970 197 283
⏲
American Express/Diners Club not accepted
The former wardrobe mistress at BBC Pebble Mill, Anne Marie Morel has now set up her own business doing alterations, trimming hats, and dyeing shoes and clothes from her mobile dressmaking tardis. Having worked on the garments for thousands of TV shows her expertise is unquestionable, as is her limitless knowledge of where to find all the best bits and pieces for any special requests.
Mail-order: By post or phone.

Sew Stylish
Unit 6
70–76 Alcester Road South
Kings Heath
Birmingham B14 7PT
Tel: 0121 444 5385
⏲ Mon & Tue 9.30–4, Thur & Fri 9.30–5, Sat 9.30–1. Closed Wed.
Cash and cheques only
This one-woman company specializes in ladies alterations. Pricing for all but the most basic changes depends on consultation with seamstress Josie Foulsham. It is best to phone first.

BRISTOL

Sirens in BS8
BS8 (Shopping Arcade)
34 Park Street
Bristol BS1 5JG
Tel: 0117 922 0223
⏲ Mon–Sat 10–5.30
Primarily an evening wear specialist, this shop within a shop will alter any style of garment at a very reasonable price.

DUBLIN

Alteration Centre
28 South Anne Street
Dublin 2
Tel: (00 353) 1 677 6258
⏲ Mon–Sat 9–6
American Express/Diners Club/Laser/Switch not accepted
Eamonn Corrigan states that what sets his shop up there among the best are his staff, who were all originally tailors and between them possess 150 years of experience in the tailoring industry. His philosophy centres on the happiness of his customers, who always come back for more. He believes in giving customers what they want, but if they request the impossible he'll refuse the service rather than risk ruining a garment. The regularly re-furbished showroom has three fitting rooms and mirrors. If a customer is not happy with their newly altered item, they can have it done again for free. A specialist in both ladies and gents alterations in fabrics including suedes and leathers.

Alterations X Press
7 South Anne Street
Dublin 2
Tel: (00 353) 1 671 7813
⏲ Mon–Fri & Sat 8.30–6, Thur 8.30–7.30
American Express/Diners Club not accepted
Highly recommended by Brown Thomas, the Harrods of Dublin, this small upstairs shop with an old-fashioned feel will alter just about anything, men's, women's or children's. All the staff are trained specialists and any garment that the customer is not satisfied with will be altered again free of charge.

GLASGOW

Clark Thomas (Tailors)
994 Pollokshaw Street
Glasgow G41 2HA
Tel: 0141 632 0469
Fax: 0141 636 5328
e-mail: clark@glasgo.demon.co.uk
⏲ Mon–Fri 9–5.30, Sat 9–1
American Express/Diners Club not accepted

This gentleman's tailor is great for women's alterations. Just walk in for a fitting or send garments with instructions by post. Clark Thomas is also a specialist dry-cleaners that will confidently deal with your delicates and beaded garments, using a high-quality hand finish. A leather and suede service is also provided.
Mail-order: Basic alterations by post take about 7–10 days. Postage and packing extra

LEEDS

Alter 8
22 Central Road
Leeds LS 1 6DE
Tel: 0113 245 3033
Mon–Sat 8.30–5.30
American Express/Diners Club/Switch not accepted
This team of trained seamstresses will alter almost anything but specialize in leather.

LONDON

First Tailored Alterations
85 Lower Sloane Street
London SW1
Tel: 020 7730 1400
Fax: 020 7730 7008
Mon–Sat 9–6
Cash and cheques only
An emphasis on quality and accuracy has led this busy shop to be regarded as one of the best in London. A staff of master tailors and couturiers deal with everything from the most basic to major alterations and repairs. Complete size reductions and enhancements are a speciality. Most fabrics, including leather, suede and sheepskin, are possible, and there is a great re-lining service.
Mail-order: Garments can be posted with instructions

Invisible Menders of Knightsbridge
161 Gloucester Road
London SW7
Tel: 020 7373 0514
Fax: 020 7373 0514
Mon, Tue, Thur, Fri 9–6, Wed 9–8, Sat 9–4
Cash and cheques only
No matter what the fabric, this is the place to go in London for invisible mending. Leathers and suedes are no problem. High-quality alteration, repair and made-to-measure services are also available.
Additional branches: Alterations, repairs and specialist dry-cleaning services at Queen's Gate Cleaners, Old Brompton Road. Tel: 020 7373 0525

F Locke / Mayfair Embroidery
33 Rathbone Place
London W1P 1AD
Tel: 0171 636 0574
Fax: 0171 636 9221
Mon–Fri 9–5
Cash and cheques only
You really couldn't do better for hand embroidery and beading than the company chosen by the couture dress designers. Allow at least a week for hand embroidery and beading services. An additional design service is available.
Mayfair Embroidery is part of the same company; initials and monograms can often be done while you wait.
Mail-order: Garments can be posted with specific instructions.

MANCHESTER

James Personal Tailor
(See tailors)

NEWCASTLE

Jules B
50–54 Acorn Road
Jesmond
Newcastle NE2 2DJ
Tel: 0191 281 7855
web-site: www.julesb.com
Mon–Thur & Sat 9–5.30, Thur 9–7.30
Diners Club not accepted
Julian Blades, winner of FHM Top Retail Designer of the Year 1999, comes from a long family tradition of tailoring. At his Acorn Road workshop, four full-time seamstresses – who are used to meeting the standards of top designers – provide quality alteration services. A first-class valet service is also available.

SHOE REPAIRS

BIRMINGHAM

AW Griffiths
319 Slade Road
Erdington
Birmingham B23 7SX
Tel: 0121 373 3612
Mon–Fri 7.45am–8.30pm, Wed 7.45–1, Sat 7.45–5
Cash and cheques only
Now in its fourth generation, this friendly cobbler's has a loyal following and high standards.

BRISTOL

The Clifton Cobbler
24 Princess Victoria Street
Clifton
Bristol BS8 4BU
Tel: 0117 974 4226
Fax: 0117 974 4226
Mon–Sat 8.30–6
Cash and cheques only
They do things the old-fashioned way here; Wayne Jenkins is most likely to be found with a mouthful of tacks spluttering 'there's no such word as no', even if complete restructuring of your best-loved shoes is the only answer. The Clifton Cobbler specializes in high-quality leatherwork with a hand-grooved, hand-stitched finish.

Ted Starzec
18 High Street
Keynsham
Bristol BS18 1DQ
Tel: 0117 9872281
Mon–Fri 9–5.30, Sat 9–5
Ted Starzec is a cobbler dedicated to his trade, whose emphasis is on workmanship and quality.

LEEDS

Tom Craggs Ltd
5 Austhorpe Road
Crossgate
Leeds LS15 8RQ
Tel: 0113 232 8304
Mon–Sat 8–5
American Express/Diners Club not accepted
With over 56 years in the business, Tom Craggs is dedicated to quality at reasonable prices.

LEEDS (YORK)

Cox of Yorkshire
30–32 The Shambles
York YO1 7LX
Tel: 01904 624449
e-mail: mail@coxofyorkshire.co.uk
web-site: www.coxofyorkshire.co.uk
Mon–Sat 8.30–5.30, Sun 11–4
American Express/Diners Club not accepted
Cox of Yorkshire is a well-established traditional cobbler's with a very professional modern approach. Also a specialist leather and sheepskin retailer, Cox's commitment to quality extends to boots, handbags and leather garment repairs and alterations.

LONDON

Mayfair Cobblers
4 Whitehouse Street
London W1
Tel: 020 7491 3426
Fax: 020 7491 3426
Mon–Fri 8–6, Sat 9–1
The choice of top shoe designer Jimmy Choo, the Mayfair Cobbler is no stranger to international and royal orders. J Holmes, the man responsible for shoe repairs, has over 40 years experience and provides many specialist services, including re-welting, re-dying, re-making, ladies' boot fittings, as well as shoe, handbag and suitcase repairs.

Scriveners Shoe Repairs
243 Portland Road
London SE25
Tel: 020 8654 7058
Mon, Tue, Thur, Fri 8.30–5.30, Wed 10–4, Sat 9–5
Cash and cheques only
This is the place to go if you'd like your shoes repaired by the President of The Society of Master Shoe Repairers. Using the best tools for the job, skills old and new have satisfied customers for over 40 years.

NEWCASTLE

Hudson Shoe Repairs
10–12 Railway Street
Northshields
Newcastle NE29 6QD
Tel: 0191 257 0040
⌚ Mon–Sat 9–5
Cash and cheques only
This cobbler's comes highly recommended for its personal service, and when we say personal we mean personal. Tea is served to waiting customers and if for a legitimate reason you are unable to collect your shoes, Bob or David will happily drop them off on their way home. With over 70 years cobbling experience between the staff, the level of quality at Hudson equals the customer service.

E Macklow
10 Brinkburn Avenue
Gateshead
Newcastle NE8 4JT
Tel: 0191 420 0407
⌚ Mon, Wed, Fri 8.30–5.30, Tue & Thur 10–5.30, Sat 8.30–12.30
Two generations after Edwin Macklow established the business in 1949, Mark Edwin Macklow maintained the family's high reputation by winning Young Cobbler of the Year for two years running in 1994 and '95. The oldest cobbler's in Gateshead is still going strong with orders coming from as far away as Hong Kong.

BUTTONS, TRIMMINGS AND HABERDASHERY

BIRMINGHAM

The Birmingham Rag Market
Edgbaston Street
Birmingham B5 4QJ
⌚Tues, Fri, Sat
For great deals in fabrics, buttons and trimmings

BRISTOL

The Great Western Antiques Market
Brunel Centre
near Temple Meads station
For information phone 0117 925 4980
⌚ Alternate Sundays
Come here for some truly unusual buttons.

BRISTOL (BATH)

Jessie's Button Box
Bartlett Street Antique Centre
Bath BA1 5 EY
Tel: 0117 929 9065
Fax: 0117 927 2608
⌚ Mon–Sat 9.30–5.30
American Express/Diners Club not accepted
Jessie is a complete button enthusiast. She regularly travels the world looking for buttons to bring back to her shop. Her enormous stock fills not only the shop but also various old cars. As well as being a collectors' paradise this is heaven for the amateur dressmaker. While some buttons are great rarities, the majority are reasonably priced, starting at only a few pence. Interesting styles range from kitsch children's plastic to chic mother-of-pearl.

BRISTOL (TAUNTON)

Fine Fabrics of Taunton
(See Fabric shops)

DUBLIN

The Leinster Button Company
93 College Orchard
Newbridge
Co Kildare
Tel: (00 353) 1 453 6366
Fax: (00 353) 045434560
⌚ Mon–Sat 9–5
Cheques only
Primarily a mail-order service, although local customers can call at the back of the house from where the business is run, the Leinster Button Company dyes and covers buttons at extremely reasonable prices. What's special about this company is that they have no minimum order; anything from 2 to 1000s of buttons can be dyed or covered. Orders will be dealt with the day they are received. Covering from 17p–85p per button, dyeing – standard £4 charge plus postage and packaging.

L M Ruban
Westbury Mall
Dublin 2
Tel: (00 353) 1 677 0791
Fax: (00 353) 1 295 4661
⌚ Mon–Sat 10 –6, Thur 10–7
Switch not accepted
This compact store specializes in everything you might need to trim and update an old favourite. Trimmings include laces, fake furs, beaded fringes, floral trims, braids and ribbons. A change of buttons will surely be found from an ever-expanding range, including some designer specialities. Mail-order: A swatch of fabric can be sent and matched to trimmings and buttons. If in stock the order will be sent out the same day as received.

The Woollen Mills
46 Wellington Quay
Dublin 2
Tel: (00 353) 1 677 0835
⌚ Mon –Fri 9–5.30, Sat 9–5
American Express/Diners Club/Switch not accepted
This family business stocks all kinds of buttons, as well as a wide selection of trimmings, ribbons and linings. Additional branches: Phone for details. Mail-order: Phone for the catalogue. Delivery time 2–3 days within Ireland, up to 7 days elsewhere.

GLASGOW

Shanazia
8–10 Albert Drive
Glasgow G41 2PE
Tel: 0141 423 5966
Fax: 0141 423 2444
⌚ Mon, Tue, Wed 11.30–7, Sat-Sun 11.30–7.30, Closed Thur
Shanazia, with four Glasgow branches, stocks over 200 button styles and a multitude of trimmings, including velvet ribbon, braids and sequins. The shops also have a wide range of fabrics, including silks and a selection of French and Austrian laces. Additional branches: Phone for details.

LEEDS

RL & CM Bond
93–97 Town Street
Farsley
Pudsey LS28 5HX
Tel: 0113 257 4905
⌚ Wed–Sat 9–4.30
Cash and cheques only
This husband and wife run shop has to be seen to be believed. With a reputation that has brought it features on Yorkshire TV, and mentions in the national press, the shop is absolutely bulging with buttons, haberdashery and trimmings. The Bonds have been trying to retire for years but demand just won't let them. With such variety and almost silly prices it is easy to see why.

Dutton's For Buttons
31 County Arcade
Victoria Quarter
Leeds LS1 6BH
Tel: 0113 245 1434
⌚ Mon–Sat 9–5.30
American Express/Diners Club not accepted
Dutton's for Buttons is brimming with brilliant buttons of every conceivable size, shape, colour and material. Dutton's even supplied the buttons for Madonna in the film *Evita*. Between them the company's five shops stock over 10,000 styles collected by the owner from all over the globe. Additional branches: York, Ilkley, Keighley, Harrogate. Phone for details. Mail-order: Phone or send fabric samples and details with SAE.

Samuel Taylor
10 Central Road
(behind Rackhams, Briggate)
Leeds LS1 6DE
Tel: 0113 245 9737
Fax: 0113 234 0726
⌚ Mon–Sat 9–5.30 (Wed 9–5)
web-site: www.samueltaylordirect.co.uk
American Express/Diners Club not accepted
Describing itself as a real Aladdin's cave of colour and excitement for the sewing and needlecraft enthusiast, Samuel Taylor is the type of place you'll find a bit of everything. Whether you're after fabrics, trimmings or buttons it's worth popping into one of the shops.
Additional branches: Leeds LS7, Harrogate, Wakefield, Huddersfield, Skipton. Phone 0113 245 9737 for details.
Mail-order: By post from Samuel Taylor Direct, 380 Meanwood Road, Leeds LS7 2JF.
By phone via the branches or through the secure credit card ordering on the web-site.

LONDON

Barnett & Lawson Trimmings
16–17 Little Portland Street
London W1
Tel: 020 7636 8591
⌚ Mon–Fri 9–5
Cash and cheques only
Stocks include braids, tassels, feathers and beaded fringes as well as lots of buttons. If they haven't got what you are after, then they'll happily get it in.

The Bead Shop
21a Tower Street
London WC2
Tel: 020 7240 0931
⌚ Mon 1–6, Tue–Fri 10.30–6, Sat 11.30–5
A dazzling array of beads spread over two floors. The majority of beads are glass but styles also include semi-precious, horn and wooden beads. Wholesale quantities and prices are available to the public from the basement range. Catches, silk threads and thonging are also available.
Mail-order: Order catalogue (£3) by phone or post

The Button Queen
19 Marylebone Lane
London W1
Tel: 020 7935 1505
Fax: 020 7935 1505
⌚ Mon–Wed 10–5, Thur & Fri 10–6, Sat 10–4
Whoever you are, and whatever your button-need, it would be hard not to find what you are after at The Button Queen. The shop carries buttons new and old in various materials – horn, pearl, leather, wood – and it's unlikely you won't find something to suit both your outfit and budget.

Celestial Buttons
54 Cross Street
London N1
Tel: 020 7226 4766
Fax: 020 7226 4766
⌚ Mon–Sat 10.30–6.30
This shop specializes in a huge range of modern buttons in styles from shirt to designer. Materials include hand-pressed glass, shell, leather and a big range of horn tailoring buttons. The ribbon and braiding extension is well worth a look if it's trimmings you are after.

V.V. Rouleaux
54 Sloane Square
London SW1
Tel: 020 7730 3125
Fax: 020 7730 3468
⌚ Mon–Sat 9.30–6, Wed 9.30–6.30
Diners Club not accepted
V.V. Rouleaux is an amazing shop, which manages to stock a terrific variety without becoming the least bit cluttered. Great lines include beaded, feathered, sequinned and tasselled trims. Ribbons, including antique, are not only available in every colour and fabric imaginable, some come with a wire edge, giving them scuptable possibilities. From long fringes to sequinned yarns, trimmings are available to enhance any wardrobe, no matter what the ethnic or historic inspiration of the moment.
Additional branches: 67 Marylebone High Street. Phone 020 7730 3125 for details.
Mail-order: International sampling service. Minimum order £10. Send SAE and description for samples.

Temptation Alley
361 Portobello Road
London W10
Tel: 020 8964 2004
Fax: 020 7727 4432
e-mail: sam@temptat.demon.co.uk
⌚ Mon–Sat 10–5.30
Primarily known for its trade services, Temptation Alley has probably the most comprehensive and unusual trimmings collection in the country. Recent projects have included films such as *Brave Heart* and *Shakespeare in Love*. Stocks include exclusive ranges unavailable to the public elsewhere. If any further style qualification is required, the owner is the ex-fashion editor of Hong Kong *Tatler*. Buttons can be dyed to match. A large range of feathers and feather trims are available.
Mail-order: Phone, post and e-mail for sampling service

MANCHESTER

The Trimming Shop
6 Manchester Chambers
Oldham
Tel: 0161 628 7080
⌚ Mon–Sat 9–5
American Express/Diners Club not accepted
This mother and daughter business is crammed to the rafters with trimmings, laces, sequins, beads and lots of helpful advice. Buttons are a speciality with over 3,000 in wood, mother-of-pearl, metallics and diamanté.
Mail-order: No catalogue, but orders can be made using swatches of fabric to match.

NEWCASTLE

W Boyes & Co.
Blackwellgate
Darlington DL1 5PW
Tel: 01325 460951
Fax: 01325 369498
⌚ Mon–Sat 9.30– 5.30
Cash and cheques only
The biggest haberdasher in the North /North East, with a total of 24 branches, Boyes sells from a stock of thousands of loose and carded buttons and a diversity of trimmings, under the slogan 'Boyes for good value.'

FABRIC SHOPS

BIRMINGHAM

Barry's Fabrics
59 Edgbaston Street
Birmingham B5 4 QJ
Tel: 0121 622 6102
⌚ Mon–Sat 9.30–4.30. Closed Wed.
American Express/Diners Club not accepted
With the same owner (Barry Leon) as Leon's of Manchester, Barry's stocks a huge range of fabrics. The slogan of both stores is '1000s of rolls at reasonable prices', from basic classics to more daring designs. Barry's has been used by theatre and television wardrobe departments for years.

The Fancy Silk Store
27 Moat Lane
Birmingham B5 5BD
Tel: 0121 643 7356
Fax: 0121 643 8846
⌚ Mon–Sat 9–6
The name is slightly misleading: the shop actually stocks everything from fashion basics to lycras, nets, snakeskins and unusual sealed sequins.The Fancy Silk Store is another favourite of the theatre and television wardrobe departments and was even used by The Bolshoi Ballet and the Russian State Circus when they came to town.

Soho Road
Many shops in this area have wonderful silks and sari fabrics.

BRISTOL (TAUNTON)

Fine Fabrics
Magdalene Lane
Taunton TA1 1SE
Tel: 01823 270986
Fax: 01823 270986
e-mail: stitcher@rmplc.co.uk
web-site: www.needlecraft-online.com
⌚ Mon–Sat 9.30–5.30
This husband and wife partnership, staffed by 13 knowledgeable employees, offers a huge range of fabrics, buttons and haberdashery. Stocking more than 2,000 fabric rolls, 2,000 button types and countless

trimmings, Fine Fabrics is one of the major stockists in the area.
Additional branch: Bridgewater. Tel: 01278 427244
Mail-order: Via web, e-mail, post and phone. Will also export. Allow 28 days but if the product is in stock it will be sent out the same or next day.

DUBLIN

The Cloth Store
67 Main Street
Blackrock
Co Dublin (3–4 miles from Dublin city centre)
Tel: (00 353) 1 288 4996
⌚ Wed–Fri 10–5, Sat 10–1
American Express/Diners Club not accepted
The Cloth Store stocks an exciting range of top-quality fabrics including Armani, Valentino, Ungaro, Paul Costelloe and Chanel. It is a women's-only specialist in both day and evening wear fabrics, from wools, linens and cashmeres to organzas and silks. Since only very small quantities – often as minute as 1 or 2 suit lengths – are stocked, this is the place to go for exclusivity. The owner, formerly a designer herself, will also advise you on the best places to go for dressmakers and alterations.
Mail-order: Phone for details. Next day delivery within Ireland; elsewhere up to 5 days.

Kevin & Howlin Ltd
31 Nassau Street
Dublin 2
Tel: (00 353) 1 677 0257
⌚ Mon–Sat 9–5.30
American Express/Diners Club not accepted
Kevin & Howlin is the only place left in Dublin selling tweed by the metre. Tweeds and only tweeds are available in pure wool or a wool/cashmere/mohair mix. These tweeds are all hand-woven in the cottages of Donegal and are therefore only available in a narrow (75cm) width.
Mail-order: If you have visited the shop you can write for specific samples.

Murphy Sheehy and Co.
14 Castle Market
(off South William Street)
Dublin 2
Tel: (00 353) 1 677 0316
⌚ Mon–Fri 10–5.30, Sat 10–5
This popular, old-fashioned shop has been in the family for three generations and has accumulated a wide-ranging clientele that includes theatre companies as well as the high street shopper. Fabrics include Irish linens, tweeds, sequinned and spangly fabrics, canvas, calicos and velvets, designer fabrics and dance wear. The majority of fabric is obtained through clothing manufacturers so stock changes from week to week. Most fabrics are remnants or roll-ends, so you are unlikely to see anyone else in your fabric.
Mail-order: Samples can be forwarded by post after a phone conversation with Jane Adam.

GLASGOW

Mandors
Fleming House
134 Renfrew Street
Glasgow G3 6ST
Tel: 0141 332 4221
Fax: 0141 332 4021
⌚ Mon–Fri 9.30–6, Sat 9–5.30, Sun 1–5
web-site: www.mandors.co.uk
Diners Club not accepted
Mandor's recently extended and renovated premises covers 10,000 ft and is packed to the brim with Italian brocades, Dutch and French fabrics, trimmings, cords, buttons, beads and sequins, to name but a few. The shop carries its own range of specially imported silks ranging from plain but vibrant colours to a new line in Celtic designs. The shop also specializes in bridal laces and silks.
Mail-order: By phone, post or web-site. Samples can be sent to match with stock. Turnaround is about 1 week.

Southside
Many shops in this area have fabulous silks and sari fabrics.

LEEDS

Samuel Taylor
(See Buttons, trimmings and haberdashery)

Whaleys (Bradford) Ltd
Harris Court
Great Horton
Bradford BD7 4EW
Tel: 01274 576718
Fax: 01274 521309
⌚ Mon–Fri 8.30–4.30 (closed 12–1)
web-site: www.whaleys-bradford.ltd.uk
This is primarily a mail-order company but customers are welcome to visit. Either way there is a minimum order of 1 metre. Whaleys specialize in natural fabrics (cottons, linens, silks) in their natural state, ideal for dying and printing. They also stock some coloured fabrics and some synthetics.

LEEDS (YORK)

York market at Newgate is open daily for fabric bargains.

LONDON

Borovick Fabrics
16 Berwick Street
London W1
Tel: 020 7437 2180
Fax: 020 7494 4646
⌚ Mon–Fri 8.15–6, Sat 8.15–5
Cash and cheques only
London's oldest theatrical supplier has been serving the wardrobes of theatre, television and film for an eternity. The shop's two floors are crammed with fabric, some traditional and some more specialist, including PVCs, fake furs and velvets.
Mail-order: A huge range of fabrics is available via an international sampling service. Send an SAE and detailed description or phone to make a debit card payment.

The Cloth Shop
290 Portobello Road
London W10
Tel: 020 8968 6001
⌚ Mon–Sat 10.30–6
While this shop is known for its ever-changing stock, it's the fabulous Indian fabrics that are a popular, constant draw. Other interesting lines include muslins and antique fabrics.

Joel & Son Fabrics
75–81 Church Street
London NW8
Tel: 020 7724 6895
⌚ Mon–Sat 8.30–5
Diners Club not accepted
All those in the know go to Joel & Son for their fabrics, which are all of top quality at very affordable prices. Specialities in the choc-a-bloc store include couture, evening and suiting fabrics and a range of beautiful silks. The comprehensive range includes 400 laces, over 500 silks and more than 100 suiting types.

MacCulloch & Wallis
25–26 Dering Street
London W1
Tel: 020 7629 0311
e-mail: macculloch@psilink.co.uk
web-site: www.macculloch-wallis.co.uk
⌚ Mon–Fri 9–6, Thur 9–7, Sat 10.30–5
This long-established store tucked in the heart of the West End carries one of the most comprehensive fabric collections in London. There are laces from across Europe and the Far East, silk dupion in over 400 colours, Swiss cottons and all manner of other fabrics. The shop also stocks an extensive range of haberdashery items, masses of trimmings and over 500 button styles. More unusual items include clear bra-straps and corset-making materials. The millinery department upstairs stocks a vast variety of hat-making materials and trimmings. Hat blocks can be bought or hired. Take a look at their web-site for a database of related fashion services.
Mail-order: International mail-order service. Phone or see the web-site for information.

Soho Silks
24 Berwick Street
London W1
Tel: 020 7434 3305
Fax: 020 7494 1705
⌚ Mon–Fri 8.30–6, Sat 8.30–5
Three floors displaying the more unusual side of the fabric world, including futuristic, PVCs and shine-in-

the-dark fabrics. Trimmings also lean towards the unusual, with fun beading and metallic laces. There is also a wide range of more traditional and upmarket fabrics and of course lots of silks.
Mail-order: Send SAE with good description. Samples will be kept as a customer record for future reference.

MANCHESTER

Abakham Ltd
11–115 Oldham Street
Manchester M4 1LN
Tel: 0161 839 3229
Fax: 0161 839 3339
e-mail: promo@abakham-fabrics.co.uk
⏲ Mon–Sat 9.30–5.15
American Express/Diners Club not accepted
Carrying a range of approximately 4,000 fabrics, 4 tonnes of remnants, at least 500 button styles and extensive trimmings and haberdashery supplies, Abakham stocks just about everything you might possibly need.
Additional branches:
Birkenhead. Tel: 0151 652 5195
Liverpool. Tel: 0151 207 4029
North Wales. Tel: 01745 562 100
Mail-order: No catalogue but samples to order service available. Delivery within two days if in stock. Up to 28 days if not in stock.

Batcher's of Manchester
58 High Street
Manchester M4 1EA
Tel: 0161 832 52602
Fax: 0161 832 6040
⏲ Mon–Sat 9–5.30
This very friendly two-floor shop is an excellent all rounder, stocking stacks of fabrics at good prices as well as a variety of buttons and trimmings. It is used by Granada TV and various theatre companies.
Mail-order: By phone, post or fax. Allow 24–48 hours for delivery.

Bennett Silks
Tel: 0161 476 8600
Fax: 0161 480 3585
e-mail: sales@bennett-silk.co.uk
web-site: www.bennett-silk.co.uk
⏲ Mon–Fri 9–5
If you're after silk then Bennett Silks will have it. Choose from a range including damasks, chiffons, satins, organzas, tartans, brocades, velvets, tussore silks, metallics...the list goes on and on. Comprehensive is the only way to describe Bennett Silks, a company where you'd be hard pushed for them not to have the colour, the type or the print for you. Contact head office (above) and they will let you know your nearest stockist. It must be stressed that silks cannot be purchased from them direct!

Leon's
419 Barlow Moor Road
Chorlton
Manchester M21 8ER
Tel: 0161 881 7960
Fax: 0161 860 5434
⏲ Mon–Sat 9.30–4.30, Thur 9.30–8
American Express/Diners Club not accepted
Leon's, under the same ownership as Barry's Fabrics in Birmingham, stocks a huge range. The slogan of both stores is '1000s of rolls at reasonable prices' and this just about sums the company up. Leon's has been used by theatre and television wardrobe departments for years.

Altrincham market and **Longsight market** are open daily for fabric bargains.

SECOND-HAND AND PREMIUM CHARITY SHOPS

BIRMINGHAM

The Birmingham Rag Market
Edgbaston Street
Birmingham B5 4QJ
⏲ Tue, Fri & Sat 9.30–4
Various stalls. One of the best areas for vintage/retro styles, and antique clothes and jewellery.

Oxfam
95 Corporation Street
Birmingham B2 4UG
Tel: 0121 236 7376
⏲ Mon–Fri 9–5.30
This shop regularly receives names from the top end of the high street and occasional couture labels such as Escada, Lorel and Whistles.
Additional branches: a smaller but similar selection is available at Oxfam, High Street, Harborne. Tel: 0121 426 5222

Yoyo
7 Ethel Street
Birmingham B2 4BG
Tel: 0121 633 3073
⏲ Mon–Sat 10–6, Sun 12–4
Yoyo is no rummage box, and at first glance you might even wonder whether it is a second-hand shop. Garments are personally selected by the owner on regular trips to the States, then laundered and repaired before being sized and hung in colour blocks. While the style is American, the atmosphere is definitely UK 2000, with an industrial decor and hip-hop, trip-hop sounds. If you like your trousers wide you can choose from boot-cut, flared and bell-bottomed Levis or cords. Leather, denim and suede jackets and bags are also very good buys.

BRISTOL

Oxfam
68 Queen's Road
Bristol BS8 1NB
Tel: 0117 925 7175
⏲ Mon–Sat 9.30–5.30
This shop has a great Oxfam Originals retro section. The range is usually 90 per cent genuine 1960s and '70s labels, 10 per cent retro style.

Oxfam
11 Regent's Street
Clifton
Bristol BS8 4HW
Tel: 0117 973 9684
⏲ Mon–Sat 9.30–4.30
This premium quality shop consistently stocks great designer bargains. Nicole Farhi is a regular name and Dior, Jean Muir, Vivienne Westwood, Katherine Hamnett and Jil Sander have all made their appearance. When we popped in there was a great Chanel handbag just in. Price depends on the condition and style; a good Jil Sander suit would be around £85.

The Real McCoy
59 Park Street
Clifton
Bristol BS1 5NU
Tel: 0117 922 5376
⏲ Mon–Sat 10–5.30
The Real McCoy is a combination of original retro clothing from the 1920s–70s and contemporary club and street wear. The shop stocks all the retro classics, current labels including Religion and Disaster, as well as the bags, shoes and jewellery to accessorize either style. Prices range from £1 to £80.
Additional branches: Exeter, five times the size of the Bristol store. Dress and evening wear hire also available. Tel: 01392 410481

Sobeys Vintage Clothing
BS8 (Shopping Arcade)
34 Park Street
Bristol BS1 5JG
Tel: 0117 940 2700
⏲ Mon–Sat 10–6
This second-hand retro shop is very big on trousers (both women's and men's cuts) and is now also moving into new

street wear. Styles include work shirts, flares (new and old, from £15–£30), and body warmers.

Uncle Sam's
54a Park Street
Clifton
Bristol BS1 5JN
Tel: 0117 929 8404
⏲ Mon–Sat 10–5.30
American Express/Diners Club not accepted
As you might expect, Uncle Sam's specializes in American imports. The shop is a must for flared-jeaned casuals, as well as miniskirted 1970s fake fur-collared glamourpusses. There are work shirts and dragon shirts for that boyfriend re-vamp (just steer him away from the Hawaii 5-0 section)..
Additional branches: Evesham, with 500,000 ft, this branch stocks hundreds of thousands of items, often at an even cheaper price than the Bristol store. Tel: 01386 40614

DUBLIN

Harlequin
10 Castle Market
(off Drury Street)
Dublin 2
Tel: (00 353) 1 671 0202
⏲ Mon–Sat 10–6, Thur 10–7
July, August, Dec open 7 days a week
American Express/Diners Club/ Switch/Laser not accepted
Owner Susan's philosophy is that she only stocks items that are to her liking. With her knowledge of the 1970s (being of that era) combined with her daughter's modern and innovative ideas, they have developed a very trendy shop which has sold clothes to the likes of Naomi Campbell, Noel Gallagher and Meg Matthews, as well as earning itself a mention in *Vogue*. Holding a small selection of clothes from the 1920s–50s, the majority of stock dates from the 1960s and '70s and includes shoes, bags and hats. The décor is a blend of modern and old that is mirrored in the company ethos of taking an old item and co-ordinating it with a new one to achieve an individual look. Prices range from £5 to £120 (for a 1920s coat).

Stage II
67a Glasthule Road
Sandycove
County Dublin
Tel: (00 353) 1 280 8117
⏲ Tue–Fri 10–1, 2–5.30, Sat 10–5.30. Closed Mon.
American Express/Diners Club not accepted
Stage II is the second-hand designer shop that lives up to its promise. It stocks all the best designer labels – Gucci, Armani, YSL, Anouska Hempel, DKNY, Jean Muir, Sonia Rykiel, Gaultier and more – at less than half their original price. Undoubtedly the best of its kind in Dublin, Stage II stocks labels and only labels and does not mix its designers with the top end of the high street. Stock comes from Irish society and London sources and only the best quality pristine garments are accepted.

Jenny Vander
20–22 Market Arcade
George's Street
Dublin 2
Tel: (00 353) 1 677 0406
⏲ Mon–Sat 10–6
Switch and British cheques not accepted
Jenny Vander is an antique and second-hand specialist of immaculate quality. On the antique side the shop stocks loads of Victorian clothes. Antique fine lace tops go for around £150 and turn-of-the-century wedding dresses for anything between £120 and £350. However, where Jenny Vander really excels is its vintage clothing and accessories, mainly dating from the 1930s, '40s and '50s. If you're after beaded cardis (around £38), crepe dresses (from £45) or a crocodile-skin purse, this is the place to go. The shop consistently stocks around 80–100 pairs of shoes and is a specialist in 1950s American jewellery, with names such as Weiss, Trifari and Myriam Haskell. Handbags include 1950s printed, crocodile and suede.

Wild Child
61 South Great George's Street
Dublin 2
Tel: (00 353) 1 475 5099
⏲ Mon–Sat 10–6, Thur 10–7, Sat 10–6
American Express/Diners Club/Switch/Laser not accepted
Brother and sister William and Vivian Walsh combine genuine 1960s and '70s gear (mini-dresses, flares, gangster pants, polo tops, polyester shirts and accessories), with their own line of '70s-style T-shirts in a bustling environment that counts 1960s and '70s soul, The Beatles and The Who among its influences.
Additional branches: A second branch, opened in October 1999 at 77 Aungier Street, is a slightly more upmarket version of the original shop, where Wild Child's own-label stock has been expanded.

GLASGOW

The Address
3 Royal Exchange Court
(off 17 Royal Exchange Square)
Glasgow G1 3DB
Tel: 0141 221 6898
Fax: 0141 221 6898
⏲Tue–Sat 10–5. Closed Mon
American Express/Diners Club not accepted
Big names at a fraction of the original price are available in this warm, inviting shop tucked away in the heart of the city centre. Sharp-eyed lovers of style will find rails and rails of new and barely worn clothes from names such as Armani, Jil Sander, Prada, Versace, Max Mara and Gucci. High-fashion high street names like Whistles, Jigsaw and Kookai are also stocked. A fast turnover of stock personally selected by the owner ensures that The Address is visited and stocked by well-known celebs from across the UK. All stock is taken in on a seasonal basis, reduced in price after 2 months and kept for a maximum of 4 months. The shop prides itself on being a relaxed, low-pressure browsing environment where an honest opinion will be given every time. Customers can be put on a list to be notified when garments from a particular source or in a specified size or style come in.

Mr Ben's Retro Clothing
Unit 6, King's Court
99 King's Street
Glasgow G1 2RB
Tel: 0141 553 1936
Fax: 0141 553 1936
⏲ Mon–Sat 10–5.30, Sun 12–5.30
If a peek at the Guinness Book of Records official World's Biggest Collection of 1970s gents nylon Y-fronts is not enough to tempt you into this yellow psychedelic haven of the unusual then you must be in denial. Owner Mary Ann King is a real clothing collector (even claiming to possess an original Gucci shell-suit), and her shop certainly reflects her fetishes. From 1770s officers' coats to 1970s Cathy McGowan, there is something for all followers of the non-high street look. Mary Ann is also a cashmere specialist and has been featured in the press for her cashmere bargains. She also has a terrific eye for wonderful handbags. Prices range from £3 to £100s.
Mail-order: If specially requested.

The Glory Hole
41 Ruthven Lane
(off Byres Road)
Glasgow G12 9BG
Tel: 0141 357 5662
⏲ Mon–Sat 10.30–5.30, Sun 1–5
Cash, cheques and Switch only
Far from being a rummage box, this well laid out, nicely lit shop stocks all last season's high street names – Warehouse, French Connection, Diesel, Oasis, Whistles, Karen Millen – whether they be cast-offs or never-worn bad buys. Although 90 per cent modern, the shop also stocks 1970s suedes, leathers, mohair scarves, bags and shoes. Whether your taste is contemporary or retro, you'll find everything for a modern everyday wardrobe here in easy to find colour co-ordinated sections, all laundered, pressed (with no missing buttons) and ready to go.

Starry Starry Night Vintage Clothing
19 Dowanside Lane
Glasgow G12 9B2
(opposite Hillhead Underground)
Tel: 0141 337 1837
Fax: 0141 337 1837
⏲ Mon–Sat 10–5.30
Cash and cheques only
Starry Starry Night puts the emphasis on women's clothes, with items dating

back to the Victorian era, although the majority of space is given over to the 1970s. However, this is not to forget the shop's 1930s dresses and an impressive range of stoles, scarves, hats, gloves, jewellery and kilts. Situated in an old wooden coach house with an Alasdair Grey mural outside, the shop is as far from minimalist as is possible to imagine.

LEEDS

Oxfam
45–47 Otley Road
Headingley
Leeds LS6 3AB
Tel: 0113 275 1734
⌚ Mon–Sat 9.15–5.30
This premium quality shop is a great place to go for recent styles from the top end of the high street, with labels like French Connection, Kookai and Oasis. The shop also has an Oxfam Originals section, which specializes in retro and funky styles for the fashion-conscious 16–35-year-old market, where you'll find Levi's (£10–£15), cords, 1970s separates and leather jackets (£15–£40).

LEEDS (YORK)

Second Chance
25 Fossgate
York YO1 9TF
Tel: 01904 674008
⌚ Mon–Sat 10–4
Cash and cheques only
Second Chance specializes in perfect-condition second-hand women's wear, mainly in styles from within the last year. Established by a group of seven friends who take turns in looking after the shop, Second Chance stocks a range of skirts, tops, suits and dresses across the age spectrum. Stock is kept for a maximum of one month.

York Designer Clothes Agency
43 Fossgate
York YO1 9TF
Tel: 01904 625400
⌚ Mon–Sat 10–5
Cash and cheques only
In this warm, homely shop all the best designer names, including Armani, Versace, Escada and Mondi, are arranged according to size. The turnover of stock is very quick so it might be worth putting your name on the client list to avoid missing out on a designer bargain. It also stocks second-hand designer handbags and shoes.

LONDON

Cornucopia
12 Upper Tachbrook Street
London SW1
Tel: 020 7828 5725
Fax: 020 7828 5725
⌚ Mon–Sun 11–6
American Express/Diners Club/Switch not accepted
Focusing almost entirely on women's clothes and accessories, Cornucopia specializes in 20th-century period and second-hand garments and offers an excellent cross-section of styles, including jewellery, handbags, hats and shoes. Jackets from £25; cocktail dresses from £35; handbags from £15.

Dolly Diamond
51 Pembridge Road
London W11
Tel: 020 7792 2479
e-mail: vintaged@globalnet.co.uk
⌚ Mon–Sat 10.30–6.30, Sun 12–6
American Express/Diners Club not accepted
This is a very interesting shop, full but by no means packed with great vintage clothes, it is the perfect place to browse, and not have to rummage. The shop specializes in evening wear. All the garments hang cleaned, labelled and dated according to their style. Style connoisseurs such as Stella McCartney have been known to drop in. Dresses from £30; gowns from £65; leather coats from £55, plus masses of gloves, scarves and bags to accessorize a nostalgic look.

Oxfam Originals
26 Ganton Street
London W1
Tel: 020 7437 7338
⌚ Mon–Sat 11.30–6.30
American Express/Diners Club not accepted
The three London Oxfam Originals stores specialize in vintage, retro and funky styles for fashion-conscious 16–35-year-olds. With a few earlier exceptions, the majority of stock comes from the 1960s, '70s and '80s – you'll find Levi's, cords, separates and leather jackets. Prices are perhaps not as low as you'd expect for Oxfam but having all the interesting stuff sorted from the charity shop heap is worth paying for, and of course it is all for a good cause. Additional branches: 123a King's Road, SW3, Tel: 020 73517979; 22 Earlham Street WC2, Tel: 020 7836 9666

Sign of the Times
17 Elystan Street
London SW3
Tel: 020 7589 4774
⌚ Mon, Tue, Thur, Fri 10–6, Wed 10–7, Sat 10–5.30
American Express/Diners Club not accepted
This wonderful shop stocks only the best and most current designers, and garments are all from this or last season. Service is highly personalized and clients' preferences can be noted so they can be contacted about interesting new arrivals. An extensive range of top quality handbags, shoes and belts is carried. The mark-up is small to keep the costs down and the collection current. All garments are individually priced.

Steinberg & Tolkien
193 King's Road
London SW3
Tel: 020 7376 3660
Fax: 020 7376 3630
web-site:
www.steinbergandtolkien.com
⌚ Mon–Sat 11–7
Europe's largest vintage and designer clothes boutique is internationally famous. The shop has its own buyer in the USA and is constantly updating its amazing collection of one-of-a-kinds from the fashion houses of Dior, Chanel and Pucci, to name but a few. Garments date from the Victorian era, though the majority are from the 20th century. As well as a multitude of garments the shop has an extensive collection of costume jewellery from the 1930s to 1950s, handbags and accessories. 1950s–60s dresses from £60; 1940s–50s handbags from £65.

MANCHESTER

Pop Boutique
34–36 Oldham Street
Manchester
Tel: 0161 236 5797
⌚ Mon–Sat 9.30–5.30
Pop Boutique is more like a 1960s film set than a shop. It is a must for quirky girls into funky, outrageous retro-gear. Star buys include '70s dresses, shoes, and leathers.

Vintage Clothing Co.
Aflecks Place
Church Street
Manchester
Tel: 0161 832 0548
⌚ Mon–Fri 10–5.30, Sat 10–6
American Express/Diners Club not accepted
This is the laid-back answer to Pop Boutique's glam. The styles here are more masculine, although the shop is also popular with girls. It specializes in 1960s–80s items which can be teamed up with modern clothes for a unique look. Currently the American influence is strong, reflected in the shop's informal work-wear styles.

Oxfam Originals
98 Smithfield Buildings
Oldham Street
Manchester M1 1JA
Tel: 0161 839 3160
⌚ Mon–Sat 10–6, Sun 10–5
The only fully fledged Oxfam Originals shop outside London, this store specializes in vintage and retro gear, mainly from the 1960s, '70s and '80s. Prices are perhaps higher than you'd expect for Oxfam but having all the interesting stuff sorted from the charity shop heap is worth paying for.

NEWCASTLE

Attica
2 Old George Yard
The Cloth Market
Newcastle NE1 1EZ
Tel: 0191 261 4062
⌚ Mon–Sat 10.30–5.30
Cash and cheques only
The range of antique clothing stretches from the 1920s–70s, dispersed throughout an environment of

1950s–70s furniture within a two-storey converted stable. The bulk of the clothing dates from the 1960s, with dresses from £8.50–£20, but prices vary since everything is a one-off. Leather is a speciality, with leather coats at around £50.
Mail-order: Yes, on request.

Period Clothing
38–40 Granges Street
Newcastle
Tel: 0191 232 5514
⌚ Mon–Fri 10.30–5.15, Sat 10–5.30
Cash and cheques only
The period in question here is most definitely the 1960s and '70s. Leather coats, blouses, dresses, flares and platforms mingle with cocktail shakers, '70s lamps and other artefacts from two decades of style.

Oxfam
2 Acorn Road
Jesmond
Newcastle NE2 2DJ
Tel: 0191 281 8873
⌚ Mon 10.30–5.30, Tue–Fri 9.30–5.30, Sat 9.30–4.30
This store, in the most fashionable area of Newcastle, is classed by Oxfam as a premium quality shop. Designer and top end of the high street bargains come in all the time.

TAILORS

BRISTOL

Territo Tailoring
33a Park Street
Bristol BH1 5NH
Tel: 0117 927 3130/ 0117 940 1666
⌚ Mon–Fri 9–6, Sat 9–4
Cash and cheques only
A small tailor's shop creating made-to-measure men's and women's suits for people who look for individuality. Gioacchino (Jack) Territo, one of a dying breed of real artisan tailors, specializes in quality handwork and a truly personalized service. Expect to pay £400 to £800 for a basic wool suit.

DUBLIN

Cleary and Magee
24 Grafton Street
Dublin 2
Tel: (00 353) 1 679 8346
Fax: (00 353) 1 872 1882
⌚ Mon–Sat 10–5.30 (by appointment)
Cleary and Magee bring together the perfect combination of classic women's tailoring (Magee) and soft, fluid draping (Cleary). From their showroom-studio, the partnership tailors superbly finished garments to order. Garments can be re-created from photos and drawings, or your favourite suit can be requested in a different fabric. They also specialize in hats to complement an existing outfit or one of their new creations.

J Martin & Sons
13 Fitzwilliam Square
Dublin 2
Tel: (00 353) 1 676 4893
⌚ Tue–Wed 10–5
Superb quality tailoring has been in the blood here since 1895. Joseph Martin senior divides his time between New York, London and the company's Sligo location. Women's tailoring is limited to traditional sportswear but the company's impeccable craftmanship in a vast variety of fabrics – such as tweeds, wools, cashmeres, linens, cottons and cords – is something special for the customer who is willing to pay for the great attention to detail of this Savile Row standard bespoke tailor.

Oakes
11 South William's Street
Dublin 2
Tel: (00 353) 1 670 4178
Fax: (00 353) 1 677 0363
⌚ Mon–Fri 10–6, Sat 10–5
Niall Tyrrell and Donald Brennan are the designers behind Oakes. They have an interesting philosophy that will appeal to any woman not of model proportions. From the basis of a fresh seasonal collection, any garment can be 'customized' by changing the details, fabric, colour or proportions. As part of a very personal service, which encourages people to explore what really suits them, Oakes offers a choice of sleeve styles, as well as various fabric options. Samples can be viewed in the shop in sizes from 8 to 18. Expect to pay £470– £590 for a woman's suit, £450 for an evening dress; separates from £110–£235.

LEEDS

Elie Tailoring
43 New Briggate
Leeds LS2 8JD
Tel: 0113 243 2758
⌚ Mon–Fri 10.30–5 (by appointment)
Cash and cheques only
High-quality bespoke tailor Elie Youssef has dedicated his life to his art. The price of a suit from this artisan tailor (ladies' suits from £795) would be well justified by his immaculate standards and over 40 years experience. Also a specialist in leathers and suedes.

LONDON

Timothy Everest
32 Elder Street
London E1
Tel: 020 7377 5770
Fax: 020 7377 5990
e-mail: timothyeverest@dial.tipex.com
⌚ Mon–Fri 9–6 Sat 9–4 (by appointment)
Diners Club not accepted
Famous for a modern slant on traditional tailoring, Timothy Everest offers a full bespoke service for ladies (two-piece from £995). Since 80 per cent of the clientele is female an extensive range of fluid fabrics is available. Timothy Everest applies an impeccable approach to give women both what they want and what flatters them best.

Richard James
31 Savile Row
London W1
Tel: 020 7434 0605
Fax: 020 7287 2265
web-site: www.richardjames.co.uk
⌚ Mon–Fri 10–6, Sat 11–6
A look at the company web-site is enough to tell you that you're dealing with the cutting edge of 21st-century tailoring. Richard James tailors largely for men, but his talents extend to bespoke women's creations (two-piece from £1,350). The company's special blend of classic with modern tailoring has brought it international recognition and a cult following.

MANCHESTER

James Personal Tailor
52 Cross Street
Manchester City Centre
(above Mr Thomas Chop House)
Manchester M2 7AR
Tel: 0161 832 7678
⌚ Mon–Sat 9–5 (appointments advisable)
American Express/Diners Club not accepted
A friendly, well-established, high-quality tailor (ladies' suits from £350). Also deals with alterations.

NEWCASTLE

John Blades
Unit 2, West End Farm
Berwick Hill,
Ponteland NE20 0JZ
Tel: 01661 860281
Fax: 01661 820112
⌚ Mon–Sat 8–6.30
Diners Club/Switch not accepted
Tailoring has been in the Blades family for over 125 years. While son Julian is at the cutting edge of the trade, father John cuts impeccable quality classics (ladies' two-piece from £395). A sought-after bespoke tailor, John works in the finest Scottish tweeds and best of British fabrics. Parking and wheelchair access to the big converted barn from which he works is great.

MILLINERS

BIRMINGHAM

Brecknells Exclusive Millinery
City Arcade
23 Union Street
Birmingham B2 4SW
Tel: 0121 643 1986
⏲ Mon–Sat 9–5.30
This long-established milliners, with more than 60 years of knowledge and contacts, covers everything from a little something to wear to lunch, to the Queen's Garden Party or Ascot. This is the place to come if you're after fur in summer or straw in winter. Hats can be fitted with special bands or stretched to ensure the perfect fit. A stock of over 6,000 hats is constantly updated, featuring hats by top milliners such as Philip Treacy and Mitzi Lorenz, with prices from £15 to £500.

BRISTOL (BATH)

The British Hatter
9–11 Walcot Street
Bath BA1 5BN
Tel: 01225 339009
Fax: 01225 763617
⏲ Mon–Sat 10–5.30
Self-taught Pamela Bromley heads a small but diverse team, whose innovative ideas have earned the company a Top Five Hat Shop title from the *Evening Standard* and a feature in *Time Out*. Pamela herself specializes in daring colours and styles that do not bow to the dictates of fashion and she works only in natural fabrics. Hats from the retail stock (£65–£600) are also available to hire at half price and are always assiduously re-vamped in the studio on return.
Additional branches: Kensington, London. Tel: 020 7361 0000
Guildford. Tel: 01483 452995

DUBLIN

The Hat Studio
33 Clarendon Street
Dublin 2
Tel: (00 353) 1 679 7988
Fax: (00 353) 1 670 4799
e-mail: bepe@iol.ie
⏲ Mon–Sat 9.30–6
Behind a 1800s' shop front lies traditional quality but also a very modern collection which changes constantly as visitors from all over the world snap up the hats. This exclusive designer milliner's prides itself on its range and service. The Hat Studio offers walk-in fittings and a dye-to-order service. Prices range from £40 to £600 (average price £120).

GLASGOW

Mad Hatter
6 Cannieburn Towell
Bearsden
Glasgow G61 2QU
Tel: 0141 942 1711
⏲ Mon–Sat 10–5
You certainly don't have to be mad to hire a hat from this shop. In fact The Mad Hatter is a very sensible option for those who need the perfect hat for that special occasion and perhaps have neither the cash nor the space to make a permanent purchase. Top names include Herald and Hearts, Bailey Tomlin, Fredrick Fox (milliner to the royals), and hats are maintained at buying condition. For those with hard-to-fit heads, Sandra Phillipp's patented inner elastic sizings achieve the perfect fit. The usual hire period is Thursday–Monday (£20–£60), but special arrangements can be made if you're leaving the country. A range of casual hats is available to buy during the winter.
Additional branches: Edinburgh. Tel: 0131 315 4111

LEEDS

Get Ahead Hats
Dutton Farm (A59)
Near Hessay
York YO5 8JU
Tel: 01904 738 656
Fax: 01904 738 656
⏲ Mon–Sat (evening appointments possible, 24 hour answerphone)
Get Ahead Hats outlets stretch from the Midlands to Scotland. What makes them a bit different is that the milliners all work and sell from the farmhouse not the high street. This is not to suggest that the company is at all amateur. The whole team is trained in millinery and the company is very professional in its product and philosophy. Every outlet has its own showroom and fitting room and stocks at least 300 hats, priced from £39 to £179; Dutton Farm, run by owner Beryl Otley, has a range of over 1,500. The company prides itself on its ability to rid people of their fear of hats by giving them the time to experiment and walk away confident from head to toe. All styles can be altered to fit perfectly. Hats can be made from remnants of your outfit fabric or dyed to order. Hats are hired (£15–£45) for a maximum of three times.
Additional branches: Yorkshire, Cheshire, Lancashire, Lincolnshire, Leicestershire and Dumfries.

Hattie's Hats
Claverly House Farm
Claverly
Leeds LS28 5QJ
Tel: 0113 257 4181
Fax: 0113 257 4181
⏲ Daytime or evening by appointment (can get a hat out at midnight) 24-hour answerphone.
Hattie's is based in the owner's home so Judith North puts herself on call for any millinery emergency 24 hours a day. Hattie's maintains a stock of at least 500 hats, including names such as Genevieve Lewis and Hat Studio and catering for clients throughout the age spectrum. While the company carries the most up-to-the-minute styles, it also stores a variety of older styles, since the new season's styles do not always suit everyone. Although customers are welcome to come and browse, all fittings are by appointment and customers are asked to bring their full outfit to the fitting to achieve a perfect match. Judith North places great emphasis on consultation and likes to avoid the rule book and fit the hat to the head and the personality. Prices range from £60 to £160, or hats can be hired from £12.

LONDON

Edwina Ibbotson
45 Queenstown Road
London SW8
Tel: 020 7498 5390
Fax: 020 7498 5390
⏲ Mon–Sat 9.30–6.30 (by appointment)
Cash and cheques only
To Edwina Ibbotson line is all important. Whatever the current fashion you can be sure that her wonderful creations will be both flattering and feminine. Beautiful elegant shapes with an extra edge have become her trademark, with hats priced from around £200. Handbags and shoes can be ordered to match.

Rachel Skinner
13 Princess Road
London NW1
Tel: 020 7209 0066
Fax: 020 7209 0066
e-mail: rachel@rachelskinner.co.uk
web-site: www.rachelskinner.co.uk
⏲ Mon–Fri 10–6.30, Sat 10–1 (by appointment)
American Express/Diners Club not accepted
Rachel Skinner's accolades are numerous; her innovative creations have graced the pages of *Vogue*, *Tatler* and *Harpers & Queen*, she shows her collections twice a year at London Fashion Week, she has produced hats for television, film, and theatre, yet at her shop in Princess Road you will find a milliner still interested in creating the perfect one-off to please her customer, whoever they are. Drawing on global influences, Rachel's hats are fresh, eyecatching and elegant. Fabrics can be dyed to create a perfect match for an outfit. As well as her bespoke millinery, Rachel specializes in hair accessories and offers a seasonal ready-to-wear collection.

The millinery departments of **Debenhams** and **Harvey Nichols** are also highly recommended.

STORAGE SUPPLIES

BRISTOL

The Futon Company
1 Park Street
Bristol BS1 5PF
Tel: 0117 922 0215
🕘 Mon–Sat 10–6, Thur 10–7,
Sun 11–5
(See London)

GLASGOW

The Futon Company
Unit 2
545 Sauchiehall Street
G3 7PQ
Tel: 0141 243 2918
Fax: 0141 243 2937
🕘 Mon–Sat 10–6, Thur 10–7,
Sun 11–5
(See London)

LONDON

The Futon Company
168–169 Tottenham Court Road
London W1P 9LH
Tel: 020 7636 9984/ 020 7388 7543
Fax:020 7383 3296
🕘 Mon–Sat 10–7, Sun 11–5
This international company does a great line called design-as-you-go storage. The range includes loads of space-conscious pieces, from £9.50. Canvas-covered wardrobes come in various colours, to which you might add a canvas sweater or shoe hanger. Another great idea are Cuba Cubes, birch storage cubes that can be stacked, wall mounted, left as shelves or fitted with Cuba Drawers. If wood's not your thing there's a willow alternative. These pieces are subtle, minimalist and stylish. If you already have your bedroom kitted out you could try an underbed basket, or storage bag. For details of other branches in London and around the country, phone 020 7727 9252.
Mail-order: Phone 020 7727 9252 or write to FREEPOST FUTON COMPANY for a catalogue. No further address needed.

The Holding Company
241–245 King's Road
London SW3
Tel: 020 7352 1600
🕘 Mon–Fri 9–6.30, Sat 10–4
The Holding Company specializes in stylish, practical storage solutions, with prices beginning at £3.95. You'll find loads of amazing ideas to streamline every aspect of your life. After you've experimented with the boxes, drawer dividers, garment bags, racks, rails etc. you'll wonder how you ever got out of the house in one piece before. The range of colours, textures and styles make the Holding Company's products far more than purely functional.
Mail-order: Ring 020 7610 9160 for a catalogue or to place an order

Muji
Whiteleys Centre
Queensway
London W2
Tel: 020 7792 8283
🕘 Mon–Sat 10–10, Sun 12–6
Products are simple and functional, and won't cost an arm and a leg. We love the company's acrylic drawer cases and partitioned boxes. Other interesting ideas include lightweight fabric boxes, cardboard and translucent polypropylene storage.
Additional branches: Five in London; also in Bluewater, Kingston and Manchester

LEEDS

The Futon Company
30–32 Woodhouse Lane
Merrion Centre
Leeds LS2 8LX
Tel: 0113 245 0770
Fax: 0113 245 3663
🕘 Mon–Sat 10–6, Thur 10–7,
Sun 11–5
(See London)
Also at Clifford Street, York, Tel: 01904 655046

LEEDS (YORK)

Barnitts Ltd
24–26 Colliergate
York YO1 2BW
Tel: 01904 625601
Fax: 01904 624975
🕘 Mon–Sat 8.30–5.30
Diners Club not accepted
Check out the Domestic Department in this home and garden specialist for great storage ideas. An established family business with an emphasis on value for money, Barnitts offers many gadgets to maximize your wardrobe space and have everything ready to hand. Stock includes canvas hanging wardrobes, underbed storage, suit and dress bags, hanging shoe and sweater racks, clear plastic boxes in all shapes and sizes, free-standing rails in wood and metal, and wooden, plastic and padded hangers. Last but not least, mesh storage baskets could be the way to manage your stray beauty products.
Mail-order: If in stock the item will be sent out the same day; otherwise allow up to 28 days.

MANCHESTER

The Holding Company
41 Spring Gardens
Manchester M2 2BG
Tel: 0161 834 3400
🕘 Mon–Sat 10–6, Sun 12–5
(See London)

Muji
The Trafford Centre
137 Regent Centre
Manchester M2 2BG
Tel: 0161 747 3555
🕘 Mon–Fri 10–9, Sat 9–7, Sun 1–6
(See London)

NEWCASTLE

The Holding Company
Fenwick of Newcastle
39 Northumberland Street
Newcastle NE99 1AR
Tel: 0191 232 5100
🕘 Mon–Sat 9–5.30, Thur 9–8,
Fri 9–5.30
(See London)

INDEX

acknowledgments

S&T would like to thank the following for their help and support in turning an idea into a reality:

Al Lowman, our agent, mentor and borderline pimp, whom we love and adore
His entire workforce at Authors and Artists Group, who have worked like slaves on our behalf
Harry Stourton for introducing us to the effervescent Al
Michael Dover at Cassell for being handsome
Susan Haynes (also at Cassell) – a rare gentlewoman in the world of publishing
Maggie Ramsay, our editor – a diplomatic bag, who laughed in all the right places
David Rowley, art director at Cassell, for artistic input
Nigel Soper for his wild and witty design and slender ankles
Edward Sykes – lensman extraordinaire
Ian Atkinson – image-manipulator supreme

Next we have the workforce who pulled it together and to whom we send our love and thanks:

Natasha Bogard for organizing it all, accepting our madness and working all the hours God gave her
Abbie Gibson and her friend Sandra Dartnell for going beyond the call of duty in researching and putting together our list of vital addresses
Anne Marie at Lemonade Factory, who kept the fires burning while shooting the photographs
Conor O'Sullivan, who turned us into the other characters and deserves to win another Oscar
Pauline Hayes, who became our surrogate mum
Our friend and make-up artist Suzanne Yard, Patron Saint of the Powder Puff
All at Richard Ward hairdressers for crimping and blow-drying
Angels & Bermans for our padding and wigs
Ray Marston, the connoisseur of wigs in Britain
Anne Woodall for helping to make Rosemary look groovy
Charlie Edmonds PR for finding fabrics at a moment's notice

In addition we would like to thank all those who helped Abbie and Sandra compile our list of addresses:

Amin at BBC Pebble Mill costume store; Ian Archbold; Nada Backo (Prolific) Lynda Cleasby (*Western Daily Press*); Julie Day; Richard Free; Maxine Gordon (*Yorkshire Evening Press*); Trevor Griffith (The Society of Master Shoe Repairers); Andrew Groves; Jane Hall (*Newcastle Journal*); Wayne Jenkins; Alison Kerr (*The Glasgow Herald*); Mark Lockyer; Deirdre McQuillan (*The Sunday Tribune*); Jasmin Main (Prolific); Sue March; Anne Marie Morel; Julie Nottingham; Kathleen O'Callaghan (*Irish Independent*); Sinead O'Connor and friends; Roz Pafferson (*Daily Record*); Janet Reeder (*Manchester Evening News*); Gigi Rouse; Sol Sanchez; Agnes Stevenson (*Glasgow Evening Times*)
Fashion and Textile Departments at University of West England, University of Northumbria, Manchester Metro, Birmingham Institute of Art and Design, Leeds College of Art and Design

Other picture credits: p.9, 86,166-7: Images Colour Library; p.64-65 Science Photo Library